Honeysuckle, Honeyjuice

Books by James Liddy (to date)

Esau My Kingdom for a Drink: Homage to James Joyce on His LXXX Birthday (Dolmen Press, 1962)
In a Blue Smoke (Dolmen Press, 1964)
Blue House, with Jim Chapson and Thomas Hill (Nine Beasts Press, 1968)
Blue Mountain (Dolmen Press, 1968)
A Life of Stephen Dedalus (White Rabbit Press, 1969)
A Munster Song of Love and War (White Rabbit Press, 1971)
Baudelaire's Bar Flowers (Capra Press, 1975)
Orpheus in John French's Ice Cream Parlour (Funge Art Centre, 1975)
Corca Bascinn (Dolmen Press, 1977)
Comyn's Lay (hit & run press, 1978)
Chamber Pot Music (hit & run press, 1982)
Moon and Star Moments (At-Swim Press, 1982)
At the Grave of Fr. Sweetman (Malton Press, 1984)
Young Men Go Walking, in *Triad: Modern Irish Fiction* (Wolfhound Press, 1986)
A White Thought in a White Shade (Kerr's Pinks, 1987)
Art Is Not for Grownups (Blue Canary Press/Kerr's Pinks, 1990)
In the Slovak Bowling Alley (Blue Canary Press/Kerr's Pinks, 1990)
Trees Warmer Than Green: Notes towards a Video of Avondale House (International Univ. Press, 1991)
Collected Poems (Creighton University Press, 1994)
Epitaphery (White Rabbit Press, 1995)
Poets in a Frieze and a Valentine (Meeting Eyes Bindery, 1999)
Gold Set Dancing (Salmon Poetry, 2000)
I Only Know That I Love Strength in My Friends & Greatness (Arlen House, 2003)
Ideas of Gold Shadows (Blue Canary Press, 2003)
Radio X-mas (Blue Canary Press, 2004)
The Doctor's House: An Autobiography (Salmon Publishing, 2004)
On the Raft with Fr. Roseliep (Arlen House, 2006)

James Liddy (r) with Hank Schlau at a Rodney, Mississippi, juke joint, May 1993.
Photo by Tomás Larscheid.

James Liddy was born in Dublin in 1934, and raised in Coolgreany, Co. Wexford. He was the prime mover behind the renowned journal, *Arena*, in the early 1960s. The Dolmen Press brought out his first poetry collection, *In a Blue Smoke*, in 1964. Since then, Liddy has published numerous books and pamphlets with a variety of distinguished presses, including *Collected Poems* (Creighton University Press, 1994). He is a professor at the University of Wisconsin-Milwaukee, and an influential scholar of Irish Studies.

Michael S. Begnal
EDITOR

Honeysuckle, Honeyjuice

A Tribute to
James Liddy

First published by Arlen House on 20 April 2006

Arlen House
PO Box 222
Galway
Ireland
Email: arlenhouse@gmail.com
Phone/Fax 086 8207617

ISBN 1-903631-71-8, paperback

Cover painting 'James Liddy 1977' by Paul Funge is reproduced with the kind permission of the artist
Typesetting: Arlen House
Printed by: Colourbooks, Dublin

contents

"Humble Homage" by Myles na Gopaleen, published with the kind permission of the Estate of Brian O'Nolan.

Letter from Charles Bukowski to James Liddy, published with the kind permission of Linda Lee Bukowski.

"The Poet as Saint" by Michael Hartnett, from *A Book of Strays* (2002), by kind permission of The Gallery Press (Loughcrew, Oldcastle, County Meath, Ireland), and Wake Forest University Press (North Carolina).

"Letter to James Liddy" by Knute Skinner, from *The Cold Irish Earth: New and Selected Poems of Ireland, 1965-1995*, by kind permission of Salmon Publishing, Cliffs of Moher, Ireland.

"James Liddy, the Priest of Poets", interview by Trent Hanson, originally published in *The Milwaukee Orbit*.

The painting 'James Liddy 1977' by Paul Funge is reproduced with the kind permission of the artist. Thanks to Paula Malone Carty for the photographic reproduction.

The support of Liam O'Connor and Nora Liddy in making the painting available to be used is very gratefully appreciated by the publisher.

Many thanks also to Liam O'Connor for the Honeysuckle motif drawn especially for this Tribute to James Liddy.

THOMAS KINSELLA

Legendary Figures, in Old Age

I saw there a number of elders
in intimate companionship,
their old shapes without shame:

playing with one another
– with all that remained
of the barbed shafts of Love.

And I heard one of them saying
to those around her:
"We cannot renew the Gift

but we can drain it to the last drop".

Delirium

the doctor halted
in his hospital coat

at the foot of my bed
in his late twenties

recently qualified
to my dazed respects

our eyes feeding
on each other

Summer Evening, City Centre

The midges were swarming
in the last light
at the end of the Lane.

A golden haze seething,
minute and furious
in their generation.

Addendum

And remember that My ways
that can seem in the short term
mysterious and unfair
and punishing to the innocent

find out and justify in the end
the searchers after truth, and not
the power-seekers, crumpled in their corner.

Genesis

It is possible the beginning might have been set
among a different people, in a farther country
at the Western boundary, near the Northern dark.

But where the growth was plenteous enough,
in their own words,
to make the herd animals burst ...

Promiscuous, the users of wicker vessels
covered in animal skins,
their stories too

were of dispossession and exile, fatal women,
honour and shame and family division,
rivalry and wrath and alien kings,

occasions and places appointed for good or evil,
and births foretold, the infants swapped or concealed.
Fate took shape and settled once among them

as a bird with black wings on a great stone.

THOMAS KINSELLA was born in 1928. The Dolmen Press published his first pamphlet in 1952, and he has gone on to become one of Ireland's most important poets. He is also noted for his translations of Gaelic poetry and of the *Táin*, and for his critical volume *The Dual Tradition*. Kinsella's *Collected Poems: 1956-1994* was published in 1996 by Oxford University Press, and reprinted by Carcanet in 2002.

John Behan

James Liddy Reminded Me of Bacchus

James Liddy introduced me to Patrick Kavanagh in the happy days prior to Kavanagh's marriage. Previous to that I had known the great poet as a performer in McDaid's, sometimes quiet and brooding, at other times raucous and loud. Being quite shy at that time I was somewhat in awe of the person of Kavanagh and had never spoken to him. In 1959/60 I had read his poetry published in *X Magazine*, a very influential arts magazine, greatly respected in London. Then the small, beautiful volume *Come Dance with Kitty Stobling* appeared. This convinced me that a major poet, after years of neglect, was at last receiving due recognition. Through that first encounter with P.K. I met his future wife Katherine and we became very friendly – there was a great sense of liberation in the air, the young poets who had no hang-ups about the past wandered in and out of McDaid's – Paul Durcan, Brian Lynch, Michael Smith, Macdara Woods, Eiléan Ní Chuilleanáin and many others – there was a celebratory mood, people sparking off each other. Little magazines like *The Holy Door*, *Poetry Ireland* and Liddy's own pet lamb *Arena*, all enlivened the scene.

James Liddy always reminded me of Pan, of Bacchus, surrounded by young poets and artists, a sense of the Greek joy in life, a moveable feast. Of course analogous to the poetry and prose, we visual artists were also beginning to flex our muscles – the Independent Artists were established since the late 50s and were a serious force within the cultural life of the country, and a group of younger artists – Charlie Cullen, Joe O'Connor, Joe Dolan, Leonde Sachy, Tadhg MacSweeney and myself formed the New Artists Group which had many exhibitions in and around St. Stephen's Green in the early 60s.

As in Paris in the early twentieth century, when "Bande Picasso", the group of visual artists around the Bateau Lavoir, and the poets Apollinaire and Max Jacobs hit off each other to produce art and poetry, so it was in 60s Dublin. No one had a bean; it was bread and water rations, washed down with Guinness. James Liddy produced a forum for poetry; it was generous and broad, inclusive, and he also bought works of art when possible. I suppose Liddy is epitomized in his poem "Patrick Kavanagh's Dublin":

We travel through Dublin's wide streets bearing
white flowers to throw in bunches to our young friends
and sunrise hallos from forgiveness to our unknowing lovers
where roof-high breezes out of a green still
on the fields pour along our hands which clumsily confess
the faithfulness too deep for anything but walking.

John Behan, Charles de Gaul airport, Paris, 3 May 2004

JOHN BEHAN was born in Dublin in 1938. He studied at the NCAD, Dublin, at Ealing Art College, London, and at The Royal Academy School in Oslo, Norway. He has participated in all major Irish exhibitions since the 1960s and has had many major commissions. John Behan's sculpture is included in numerous collections throughout the world.

DESMOND EGAN

The Hair of the Dog

The isolation of the artist in the heart of bourgeois society has never been greater, his work has never been more anonymous - George Baselitz

after the long conversation
after you saw Kavanagh home

it was time to wander off alone
half jarred on words beyond
the exhaustion of Baggot Street

you might smile at Georgian houses
they watched like wardens
the windows always had ears

your reflection moved there
torn into colour like a Bacon figure

you had to leave to live
in the university of strangers
in a room of your own
somewhere beyond Chicago
holidaying where you belonged

the loss was ours James
but you marked your way home
with poems that do not smile

DESMOND EGAN was born in 1936. He has published sixteen collections of poetry, won the Muir Award in 1983 and the American Society of Poetry Award in 1984. His Goldsmith Press published Patrick Kavanagh's posthumous autobiographical novel, *By Night Unstarred* (1977) and the biography of Kavanagh by his brother Peter (1979).

LIAM O'CONNOR

Liddy and I

I was in my early- to mid-twenties, and he was the same, but about a year older than I. He impressed me immediately as a person of great intellectual quality with a persuasive conviction in the presentation of his ideas. I learned that he wrote poetry, while I at the time was interested in painting. In a small town in the Ireland of the Fifties it was not easy to find too many who could talk knowledgeably about Lorca, Pound, Auden, Ginsberg, *et cetera*. We became very close friends and through him I got to know the world of McDaid's in the heyday of Patrick Kavanagh. We founded a magazine together, *Arena*, and were joined in this by Michael Hartnett. *Arena* made considerable impact in its short life. It ran for four issues over a period of about two years (1963-65) – an energetic, even vivacious, platform for many of the young writers of the time, as well as publishing the work of known and established writers. In this joint editorial activity Michael and I were helpers, but James was the editorial spring. It was his genius which lifted the magazine and gave it its buoyancy of spirit.

When *Arena* folded (there were no grant aid that I know of in those days) James and I spent a short period in Spain, after which he went to lecture in San Francisco State College, and later at the University of Wisconsin-Milwaukee.

A frequent visitor to his house in Coolgreany, I have seen him work constantly and energetically, producing draft after draft in the shaping of a poem. From his study at all times came the clacking noise of an old typewriter. Poetry, for those who are unaware of it, is hard work.

I know that he tries always to use words in an unconventional way, as if to push back the edges of language to find deeper expressiveness of meaning; he is never content with the easy or the glib. He has produced a succession of remarkable books, each one a development on his previous work, or a venture in a new direction. He continues working as intensely as ever, producing new poems, witty, provocative, or with a subversive religious theme. (I think he believes that all true religion is subversive – was Christ comfortable?)

Long may he continue to stimulate, entertain and enlighten us. As for myself, I have found him to be a generous and faithful friend and I treasure his existence.

LIAM O'CONNOR was born in 1936, headed Design Team in Arklow Pottery in his early years, and then worked as a graphic designer and calligrapher. Along with James Liddy and Michael Hartnett he co-edited *Arena*.

Michael Hartnett

The Poet as Saint

I thought upon this friend.
He, the rich effusive man
preaching love for love's ends,
words and metres huge as
his Christ-love for his hundredth Judas.
He is father to many poets
and he is lover of their songs.
Largesse is his forte, as well as love:
and the great energy denoting love
and the lax compassion denoting love.
We have sat in Malaga
arguing over servants' ways
mistaking love of the master
for love of what the master pays.
We have argued over style
in the grey sheltered limestone bays
of Clare and not agreed: but we
shall be poets in coming days.

Michael Hartnett (1941-1999) hailed from Newcastle West, Co. Limerick, and was one of Ireland's most celebrated poets. He wrote in both English and Irish, and also translated Gaelic poets Ó Bruadair, Ó Rathaille and Haicéad. Gallery Press published his *Collected Poems* in 2001. He co-edited the literary magazine *Arena* with James Liddy and Liam O'Connor.

James Liddy

La Muerte de Joselito

Photograph in a Córdovan bar

"Ignacio Sánchez Mejías, contemplando emocionado el cadaver de su cuñado Joselito, pocas horas después en ocurrido el fallecimiento del gran torero".

And the friends of our friends are our friends
Particularly in the spirit world known to the violent
In life or love who transform the materials.
If you solitarily emerge eventually into sunlight and logos
You find yourself garlanding the scene
The salutation of a walk on a summer's day.
What is most beautiful grows in someone else's garden
Not in the much tended flowerbed under your window.
But what force there is in the motiveless.
If you talk to children you become a father.
If you sing of someone your song is lifted by the distance.
A grief in your arms and your death is wept in the street.
A sword can throw shadows far ...
In addition, on another level the aura of spectacle
The intricate performance of dance as religion
The dancer coaxing God out of his body to be,
Suits of light make the best hearse clothes.
Stars, sequins and the colours caparisons for death.
Under a canopy of roses, limewash and orange trees
In the fall of a dark blue sky to absent minarets
The torero dancing away from us lightly
To swagger with sword in some other land
Silent rhetorician of escalation.

from *Blue Mountain* (1968)

Knute Skinner

Letter to James Liddy

[In the mid-60s, when I first knew James Liddy, he was already a one-man centre of literary activity with an enthusiastic following of young poets whom he was influencing and helping to get recognition. Our occasional meetings, celebrative – overflowing with drink and talk – often took place in his parents' summer home in Kilkee (often enough that my four-year-old son named him "Mr. Kilkee"). So in March of '66, when I returned from a three-month stint teaching in America, I looked forward to seeing James. Instead, I found a postcard he had sent from Spain: "Doing a Joyce at last". It was typical of him not to stand still, I thought, even though disappointed. And he *was* getting better weather. The following poem was written that June].

June 1966

Pray for us James; we have had
an unnatural season.
March, April and May
washed off in the rain
of our cold, flu-ridden land.
Little is in the ground
and few have gone to the bogs.

Ah James, Mr. Kilkee,
self-exiled in Spain,
"doing a Joyce at last",
what do you make of that weather?
Is it too hot for the son
of generations of Claremen?
And how is your Joyce doing?

What news would interest you now?
De Valera re-elected?

A higher tax on tobacco?
Better to mourn your ancestors
lost to these stones of Clare.
We have little to bank on here.
And the doors of the banks are shut.

Pray for us, James; write us
a poem of such dimension.
Do priests bless your typewriter there?
Then send us such words as clear
the darker cast of the sky.
Though you cannot settle the bank strike,
James, settle our souls.

KNUTE SKINNER was born in 1929 in St. Louis, Missouri, but has lived for decades in Co. Clare. Among his numerous publications is *The Cold Irish Earth: New and Selected Poems of Ireland, 1965-1995* (Salmon Publishing, 1996).

EAMONN WALL

From the El to Axel's: Irish Poets Stateside

In their introduction to *The Penguin Book of Contemporary Irish Poetry*, Peter Fallon and Derek Mahon note that the "notion of exile has for centuries permeated the Irish consciousness and while it was true for writers like Joyce and Beckett, it is hardly true in the same sense for younger poets".[1] They cite Eamon Grennan as an example of a poet who lives and works in upstate New York but who returns to Ireland for extended periods. Fallon and Mahon characterize Grennan, and writers of his generation and younger, as commuters. Continuing in this vein, Dermot Bolger in the foreword to his 1993 anthology, *Ireland in Exile: Irish Writers Abroad*, argues that the terms "*exile* and *departure* suggest an outdated degree of permanency" and that "Irish writers no longer go into exile, they simply commute".[2] A roadblock Bolger encountered while editing his anthology "was remembering who was now back [in Ireland] and who was away".[3] Fallon and Mahon point out that Irish poets "have always looked abroad" and that this is true even of those poets who have lived all of their lives at home.[4] In the contemporary period, they note "increasingly the give-and-take between Irish and American poetry, sharing as it does a comparable relationship with the English language, and determined as their countries are by transatlantic neighbourhood".[5]

Many Irish poets, across the generations, live permanently in the US, some are naturalized citizens, though they all cross the Atlantic regularly, while others have spent extended periods there: Brian Coffey, Thomas Kinsella, John Montague, Richard Murphy, James Liddy, Seamus Heaney, Seamus Deane, Eamon Grennan, Derek Mahon, Eavan Boland, Richard Ryan, Paul Muldoon, Nuala Ní Dhomhnaill, Joan McBreen, Gerard Donovan, Sara Berkeley, Greg Delanty and so on are writers who belong to this group.

However, the traffic has in no way moved in one direction: American poets have also settled in Ireland, visited Ireland for extended periods, and made Ireland part of their work. In the contemporary period alone such a list would include, though hardly be confined to, John Berryman, Robert Lowell, Theodore Roethke, Jean Valentine, Gary Snyder, Richard Tillinghast, Billy Collins, Anne Kennedy, Julie O'Callaghan, Knute Skinner, Michael Begnal, Thomas Lynch, Jessie Lendennie, and Ben

Howard. In addition, Wallace Stevens, who never visited Ireland, used Ireland as the setting for some of his most memorable later lyrics. Many of this group of Americans are not of Irish descent and have been drawn to Ireland by its poetry and not by the quest for links with their ancestors. Also, poets based in their home countries cross the ocean to give readings and workshops in Ireland and the US, where they also publish their poems in literary journals. Memoirs and biographies have detailed literary friendships between John Berryman and John Montague, Theodore Roethke and Richard Murphy, and Robert Lowell and Seamus Heaney. Internationally, the influence of both American and Irish poetry has been pervasive, and they have, in turn, influenced each other.

At the same time, for all of these connections and even with the emergence of a global world through global technologies, when the Irish poet arrives in the US or the American poet arrives in Ireland, he/she must come to terms with a new place. The jumbo jet has supplanted the coffin ship and the commuter the exile; however, despite the speed of travel, the emigrant or literary pilgrim can still encounter various levels of disjunction, and will soon learn that the text and the place are frequently out of synch. The newly-arrived Irish poet will soon be labelled as an Irish-American, a designation one may feel immediately uncomfortable with, creating as it will images of tourists in plaid trousers and green jackets marching through Dublin on St. Patrick's Day. Similarly, the American poet will be amazed by Ireland's obsession with American politics and popular culture and will be shocked, for example, to find himself stuck in a five-mile tailback emanating from an Eminem concert at an Irish racecourse. Writing of spending time in America, and of travel in general, Seamus Heaney has learned:

> Oddly enough, getting to know strange places or strange things for the first time – on holiday, say, or at work in different parts of the United States – has not usually excited the poem-writing part of me. Letters and journal entries can record that "present joy", but generally speaking, the whole thing needs to go down into the clear element of the reservoir before it can be repossessed in a poem. And this is true even if I know at the time that what I am encountering is a subject that already belongs to me.[6]

The poet's consciousness undergoes a kind of flooding in a new place, and out of this mingling of the stored with the new comes the poem. For Heaney, and for all poets, the experience of having spent time in America can often be an invisible presence in the work reappearing just as easily in a poem about, say, Viking Dublin or Mossbawn, as in a poem about

Boston or Malibu. Certainly, with regard to Heaney, as he has spent so much time in the US and not detailed this part of his experience to any great degree, the US is largely an invisible presence.

The work produced by Irish poets living in America is many-sided, full of doubleness, and difficult to summarize. At the same time, an examination of such contemporary works as John Montague's *The Dead Kingdom* (1984), Eavan Boland's *In a Time of Violence* (1994), Greg Delanty's *American Wake* (1995), Paul Muldoon's *Moy Sand and Gravel* (the Pulitzer Prize winner for poetry in 2002) and James Liddy's *Collected Poems* (1994) does show some elements of shared outlooks and methodologies, if not purpose. On the surface, Montague's *The Dead Kingdom* is hardly an American book at all. Instead, it's his reworking of the *Dinnseanchas*, or lore of place poem, detailing a journey made across Ireland from Cork to the locale of his early life in the Fermanagh-South Tyrone area. This lyric movement across Ireland to the locale of childhood is underlined for Montague by the complexity of his own origins. He was born in Brooklyn to an Irish immigrant family and returned to Ireland as a young child to be raised by his mother's family. The *Dinnseanchas* calls the poet back to the place of origins where he must register varieties of absence: estrangement, death, change wrought by time. Powerfully, Montague's journey recalls the progress of his father from Cobh to County Tyrone, made with his sons, on his return home from a lifetime spent in New York:

> A small sad man with a hat
> he came through customs at Cobh
> carrying a roped suitcase and
> something in me began to contract
>
> but also to expand. We stood,
> his grown sons, seeking for words
> which under the clouding mist
> turn to clumsy, laughing gestures.
>
> At the mouth of the harbour lay
> the squat shape of the liner
> hooting farewell, with the waves
> striking against Spike Island's grey. ("At Last")[7]

The return of the father is a reversal: the returned exile being greeted by Spike Island rather than by the Statue of Liberty in the Cork town which now houses a museum devoted to Irish emigration. Prophetically, the return of the father anticipates the return home of many of the 1980s emigrants to take advantage of the Celtic Tiger boom, though unlike Montague's father, broken by America, most did not limp home. In his examination of immigrant life in America, Montague, like many contemporary Irish-American fiction writers, highlights the hardships rather than the triumphs:

> My mother
> my mother's memories
> of America:
> a muddy cup
> she refused to drink. ("A Muddy Cup")[8]

Montague's essays reveal an abiding interest in American poetry and his own poetry; his use of the short line in particular owes much to the work of William Carlos Williams. For Montague, the *Dinnseanchas*, that most ancient of Irish poetic callings, encompasses America – a place of Irish people and, therefore, an Irish place – and an American poetic line. What he has gathered is soldered to what he has inherited.

Like Montague, Eavan Boland experienced a transatlantic childhood. Born in Ireland to a father who was a diplomat and a mother who was an artist, she spent large parts of her formative years in London and New York. As a teenager, she returned to Ireland to prepare for university, and later, to attend Trinity College, Dublin. In addition to embarking on her own career as a poet, she set out to assist other women who were possessed of similar ambitions and, as a result, has been the catalyst in generating a new Irish poetry. Her role in Ireland is similar to the role played in the US by Adrienne Rich, Denise Levertov, and Anne Sexton and her development as a poet, like Rich's, displays a movement from the closed forms of youth to the more open forms of experience. A central part of Boland's literary enterprise has been the recovery from silence of the lost lives of women, often by re-imagining them next to the beautiful objects they created. One such poem is "In a Bad Light", from the sequence opening *In a Time of Violence*, set in a museum in St. Louis displaying the work of Irish seamstresses:

> I stand in a room in the Museum. In one glass case a plastic figure
> represents a woman in a dress with crêpe sleeves and a satin
> apron. And feet laced neatly into suede.

She stands in a replica of a cabin on a steamboat bound for New
Orleans. The year is 1860. Nearly war. A notice says no comforts
were spared. The silk is French. The seamstresses are Irish.

I see them in the oil-lit parlours. I am in the gas-lit backrooms. We
make in the apron front and from the papery appearance and
crushable look of crêpe a sign. We are bent over

in a bad light. We are sewing a last sight of shore. We are sewing
coffin ships, and the salt of exile. And our own death in it. For
history's abandonment we are doing this.[9]

Greg Delanty emigrated to the US in 1986 at a time of economic downturn in Ireland, and is one a generation dubbed "the New Irish" who flocked there, legally and illegally, during that decade. In his introduction to his 1990 study, *The Irish Voice in America*, Charles Fanning explained why he had not included Irish-American poetry in his study:

> There have been few memorable Irish-American poems, especially before very recent times. The problem has been an endemic blight of programmatic melancholy or bravado that emerged from the experience and perception of forced exile. The stock-in-trade of Irish-American poetry has been the immigrant's lament for a lost, idealized homeland and the patriot's plea for Irish freedom from British oppression.[10]

However, in the revised and updated version of his study, published in 2000, Fanning celebrates "the coming of age" of Irish-American poetry resulting from "the accelerating cultural interaction between America and Ireland". He finds American poets "discovering viable Irish inflections", native Irish poets "enriching the American poetic landscape", and identifies John Montague as the primary role model for these poets.[11] "The New Irish" have played a significant role in this coming of age. They are of an educated generation of Irishmen and Irishwomen, raised at home on American popular culture, who arrived in the US not as traditional exiles, but as young writers ready to play a role in American cultural life. In *American Wake*, Greg Delanty refers to the new arrivals as "the Fifth Province", and records, in various ways, the doubleness of the emigrant's existence, both in America and in Ireland. Delanty is able to explore the US from the inside by shifting with ease from Irish to American idioms:

How were any of us wiseguy kids to know
when we mocked busloads of rotund Yanks
bleating WOW! along every hedgerow
from Malin Head down to the Lee banks,
searching for the needle in the haystack
of ancestors with names like Muh-honey-ey
or Don-a-hue,
                    that I'd one day come back
a returned Yank myself, & you'd mock me
when I let slip restroom or gas station.
You accuse me of scoffing too many hot dogs,
siding unwittingly with my Vermont physician.
Now I'm even considering daily jogs,
concerned not so much for my unhealthy state,
but the scales of your eyes reading my weight. ("The Fat Yank's Lament")[12]

Delanty's engagement with America has also a political element: one of his first public acts on becoming an American citizen, exercising his freedom granted by his new status, was to be arrested as part of a protest against the bombing of targets in Yugoslavia, and, more recently, he has played an active role in the Poets Against the War movement. Instead of the programmatic melancholy and the other stock-in-trade figures that undermined Irish-American poetry, Delanty's work exhibits a sense of the poet as insider, in both Ireland and the US.

According to Clair Wills, Paul Muldoon's emigration to the US in 1987 "could almost be described as life imitating art" and she notes that the difficulty the poet faced centred on what to bring with him and what to leave behind.[13] Quickly, Muldoon's work, in *Madoc* and *The Annals of Chile*, emphasized an intense level of engagement with the places and histories of the Americas; however, even before emigrating his work was heavy with American influence, not least the influence of Robert Frost and American popular culture. Even as a child, his imaginative range was coloured by American commonplaces that could be transposed directly into an Irish context, rural Ireland and the American West, for example,

He opens the scullery door, and a sudden rush
of wind, as raw as raw,
brushes past him as he himself will brush
past the stacks of straw

that stood in earlier for Crow
or Comanche tepees hung with scalps
but tonight pass muster, row upon row,
for the foothills of the Alps. ("Tell")[14]

The issue of what should be brought and what should be left behind is a complex one when the poet from childhood has washed in the waters of American culture, high and low. In Muldoon's case, nothing needs to be left behind. Instead, what one has inherited must be reshaped by more direct contact with its source and the result of this has been an intensification of interest in the narratives and minutiae of America. At the same time, Muldoon's work is underlined by fluidity and the carnivalesque, something that results in the free play of his work. But Muldoon is a most attentive observer of America, its wildlife in particular, an interest he shares with Eamon Grennan and Greg Delanty. Muldoon is an immigrant who has written little on the subject. Instead, he has made the leap from the centre of Irish culture to the centre of American culture, and the sense that the literatures of both places can be counted in a similar currency. Grennan has written that "mine is not really an experience of exile, and to make a subject of it would be for me a kind of emotional exploitation"[15] and this also mirrors Muldoon's relationships to the US and Ireland.

Like Grennan, James Liddy leaped headlong into America. He settled first in San Francisco in the Haight-Ashbury area during the summer of love and then, after many temporary stops in various college towns, made his home in Milwaukee where he continues to live, teach, and make a great contribution to the city's cultural and social life. Like Montague and Boland, Liddy's connections to America were established early in life: his mother was a native New Yorker who settled in Ireland; therefore, when Liddy set out for the States he was getting ready to encounter a country that had been part of his inheritance since birth. He could never feel like an exile and he has never written through the voice of one. His work continues to be unmistakably Irish to the extent that he frequently explores place and shows how it shapes personality, fine tunes feelings, and refines one's language. Always in Liddy's Irish work the poetry springs from the free play of emotion, imagination and observation; however, it is ordered by the parallel free play of landscape and voice, something made clear in "Blue Mountain", an early *ars poetica*:

> Blue mountains are of themselves blue mountains
> And white clouds are of themselves white clouds
> And there is a blue mountain, Croghan Kinsella,
> And around it there are often white clouds.
>
> Whether all things are accurately themselves
> Or modifications of each other I do not know,

But clear mornings from my bathroom window
I see white clouds and a blue mountain.[16]

Liddy's early development as a poet took place in Dublin where he co-edited *Arena* with Liam O'Connor and Michael Hartnett and came under the important influence of Kavanagh. At the same time, as he has pointed out in "Patrick Kavanagh and the Beat Generation", he was reading extensively in contemporary American poetry which was freely available in Dublin's bookshops and brought back from the bookshops of England and America by literary pilgrims.[17] Right from the start, his work was being guided by American models, a guidance that intensified when he arrived in America. To judge that Liddy's work has undergone an enormous transformation since its arrival in the States is only partially true. The shape of his work has not changed that much; in fact, one of the most interesting aspects of his work is the formal consistency it has exhibited over the years. The real changes that have taken place are to be found in Liddy's themes, ideas, contexts, and associations, all of which are derived from living in America. Like Muldoon's, Liddy's level of his engagement in American life has been so intense that it has resulted in a most original body of work.

The elements of American experience that most attract Liddy to make them his poetic themes and concerns are varied and eclectic: he is the poet of polkas, bowling alleys, bedrooms and bars who remains always the singer singing the song of the self. The urban America of his poetry – Milwaukee, in particular – is as complex as Kavanagh's Dublin and Pope's London. Often, he is out of tune with Irish America and very much in tune with Serbian, Bohemian, Czech, and Polish America. The myriad voices he hears and loves become the legendary figures in his work, none greater perhaps than Frank and Millie Olson, the guiding lights of Axel's, a bar on Milwaukee's East Side:

Let Frank and Millie pour it.
Jesus drank John and Mary Magdalene under.
He was bipure.
The Church glitters psychojukebox.
We must touch the hem of her bar rag. ("Every Evening at Axel's")[18]

Of the poets considered here, Liddy's wide American range is most easily comparable to Muldoon's and in the work of both one constantly encounters the unexpected. Both poets feed on the American present, in all of its sublime and vulgar manifestations, and all of its aspects are open for examination and celebration.

Among American poets who have lived in Ireland, the most important is John Berryman who composed the final book of his great work, *The Dream Songs*, in Dublin. Many of these poems are rooted in Irish literature, history, and sense of place. In particular, Berryman arrived in Dublin to commune with the inspirational figure of Yeats:

> I have moved to Dublin to have it out with you,
> majestic Shade, You whom I read so well
> so many years ago,
> did I read your lesson right? did I see through
> your phases to the real? your heaven, your hell
> did I enquire properly into? ("Dream Song 312")[19]

The time spent by Berryman in Ireland was quite brief compared to the length of Liddy's extended American stay; however, both poets are linked by the intensity of their experience in the new place. Berryman arrived in Ireland to confront the ghost of Yeats whereas Liddy arrived in the States to more fully engage with the mother world of contemporary poetry and the world that formed his own mother. One aspect of Liddy's work that has never been considered much is his criticism, for the simple reason that it remains uncollected. Each autumn for the past twenty years or so, he has spoken on an Irish or Irish-American writer at the American Conference for Irish Studies annual Midwest meeting and a number of these lectures have been revised and published in *Éire-Ireland*, *New Hibernia Review*, and other journals. However, many of these talks have not been published. The time is certainly ripe for the publication of a volume of Liddy's collected prose.

Today, in real time, and as a result of the emergence of various technologies, Ireland and the US are more connected than ever before. Looking at Ireland as a whole, we might begin to quantify its American parts. The poets are in continual communion and this has continued and expanded the influence and cross-pollination of both poetries: Irish poetry has its American parts and American poetry has its Irish parts. At the same time, fundamental differences are apparent. Irish poetry is pretty homogenous whereas American poetry has so many variants that it is impossible for all of the poets to stand under one umbrella. Irish poetry in English is rooted in and carries forward its indigenous language whereas American poetry has gathered up many languages, while largely ignoring its indigenous ones. And it is language, and how it has travelled, that carries with it the poet's voice.

NOTES

[1] Peter Fallon and Derek Mahon, eds., *The Penguin Book of Contemporary Irish Poetry* (New York: Penguin, 1990), xx.

[2] Dermot Bolger, *Ireland in Exile: Irish Writers Abroad* (Dublin: New Island Books, 1993), 7.

[3] *ibid.*

[4] Fallon and Mahon, xxi.

[5] *ibid.*, xxii.

[6] Seamus Heaney, "Irish Poetry and the Diaspora", *Metre: A Magazine of International Poetry* 3 (Autumn 1997): 16.

[7] John Montague, *The Dead Kingdom* (Winston-Salem, N.C.: Wake Forest University Press, 1984), 71.

[8] *ibid.*, 66.

[9] Eavan Boland, *In a Time of Violence* (Manchester: Carcanet, 1994), 8.

[10] Charles Fanning, *The Irish Voice in America* (Lexington: University Press of Kentucky, 1990), 4.

[11] *ibid.* (2000 edition), 368-69.

[12] Greg Delanty, *American Wake* (Belfast: The Blackstaff Press, 1995), 11.

[13] Clair Wills, *Reading Paul Muldoon* (Newcastle-upon-Tyne: Bloodaxe, 1998), 135.

[14] Paul Muldoon, *Moy Sand and Gravel* (New York: Farrar, Straus and Giroux, 2002), 19.

[15] Eamon Grennan, "Irish Poetry and the Diaspora", *Metre: A Magazine of International Poetry* 3 (Autumn 1997): 13-15.

[16] James Liddy, *Collected Poems* (Omaha, Neb.: Creighton University Press, 1994), 33.

[17] Liddy, "Patrick Kavanagh and the Beat Generation", in Kathleen Rettig Collins, James Liddy, and Eamonn Wall, eds., *Patrick Kavanagh – Midlands Conference Papers* (Omaha, Neb.: Creighton University Press, 1995), 30-36.

[18] Liddy, *Collected Poems*, 327.

[19] John Berryman, *The Dream Songs* (New York: Farrar, Straus and Giroux, 1969), 334.

EAMONN WALL's latest collection of poetry is *Refuge at DeSoto Bend* (Salmon, 2004). He is also the author of a collection of essays, *From the Sin-é Café to the Black Hills: Notes on the New Irish* (University of Wisconsin Press, 2000). A native of Co. Wexford, he is currently a Professor of Irish Studies at the University of Missouri-St. Louis.

Myles na Gopaleen

Humble Homage (Book Review)

Esau, My Kingdom for a Drink: Homage to James Joyce on his LXXX Birthday, by James Liddy, The Dolmen Press, 3s. 6d.

The true reviewer is rarely daunted, if only because he considers his standards of appraisal and performance immutable. Yet enlightening comment on this presentation is not easy. There are eight and a half pages for the money and it is set, the publishers say, in Janson type. A quotation, taken quite at random, may help to inform the present reader:

> You saw the water from the shore, green-bedabbled, and went on cleaning your weapons to scatter for ever the parishes of fat boozy men and crumbling anaemic women, your enemies. You made them all begin to die with Blazes Boylan, Mr. Deasy, Buck Mulligan, Fr. Conmee, the Citizen and all the shadows of the devil-soul of Ireland: you put them into your book and they became satirical caricatures and witches of hate. So you, James Joyce, loving us seriously all the time behind our backs like a father, caring for us as unmarried virgins who might die without kissing life, still walking our pavements from your books and showing us our hypocrisy and time-serving, you, comradeless, hoping as you wrote but telling none that we, in our green isle of only human snakes, should read your armoury of words and begin to live.

It is all like that – illiterate schoolboy hysteria, brashness and, where any meaning can be discerned, a total ignorance by Mr. Liddy of Joyce's work and intent. If the whole thing is intended as a joke and a jeer at Joyce and his overzealous adherents, it might merit the comment of fair enough.

But there is a sinister overtone. The commentary is preceded by a brief extract (in different-coloured ink) from the National Library episode in *Ulysses*. In this, the word Richie is spelt "Riche" and the phrase "But act. Act speech." appears as "But act. Act, speech", reducing Joyce's sentence to a meaningless botch.

Nor is that everything. In the first paragraph of the stuff the name of one of the protagonists is given as "Eglington". In charity one could dismiss this as a misprint, but Eglinton again appears as "Eglington" three pages on.

Whatever the motive for it, Mr. Liddy's eructation can provoke nothing but derision and perhaps the hope that he is young enough to get a touch of the strap from the Brothers. Meanwhile, the humblest writer may pray to God that he will be spared the class of "homage" which Mr. Liddy can produce.

M. *na* G.

MYLES NA GOPALEEN was a pseudonym of Brian O'Nolan (1911-1966), who also wrote under the name Flann O'Brien. He was author of *At Swim-Two-Birds*, *The Third Policeman*, *An Béal Bocht*, *The Hard Life*, *The Dalkey Archive*, *The Best of Myles* and others.

PHILIP CASEY

The Alter Life of Books (Homage to James)

Esau, my kingdom is a drink.

In a Blue Smoke,
Christ and Socrates smiled.
I was forever young.

Above planning permission:
Blue Mountain.

Proposal for a mega-publisher:
A Life of Stephen Dedalus.
And his White Rabbit. 1969.

O Babóg, come into Munster with me,
And print love bonds, not war bonds.

In the Blue House we are gentlemen
And generous with time.

Of all the bars in all the world,
Baudelaire had to come into mine.

In the rock pools of Corca Bascinn,
My body is mistaken for a flower.
I am the sea anemone
who knows how to party.

To the philistines on every mean street
Let it be known:
I have all the Gorey Details.

As Comyn sings his Lay,
I walk into eternity
Among the hemlock and hibiscus,
The rosebuds and the hollyhock.

I am a Bachelor of Chamber Pot Music,
a Fellow of the Tent of Many Drinks.

At the grave of Father Sweetman
I hear the old world swan
Out of James Clarence Mangan
Singing its song.

Thinking a White Thought in a White Shade,
I am in my white suit,
My birthday suit of white butterflies.

Young men should always go walking.
Mens sano in corpore sano.

After a night's drinking,
There's nothing like
A good feed of Kerr's Pinks.

Art is only for grownups
When it is noted
By the Garda Síochána.

Bowling in the Slovak Bowling Alley
I am truly happy my whole life.

In Avondale the trees
Are warmer than green:
Global village warming.

My Collected Poems
Are in full control of the Faculties.

Let my Epitaphery
Be written on Porter.

Vincey O'Rafferty
powers up his sqeezebox

For Gold Set Dancing
One more time.

I Only Know
That I Love Strength –
(The old glitter)
In My Friends
(Mad philosophy
Hurts them into song)
And Greatness,
The territory of Spicer, Burroughs,
Kerouac, Michael Hartnett.

PHILIP CASEY grew up under the spell of Croghan Kinsella, James Liddy's blue mountain, in Wexford. His collections include *The Year of the Knife, Poems 1980-1990.* and *Dialogue in Fading Light: New and Selected Poems* (New Island, 2005). His novels are *The Fabulists, The Water Star* and *The Fisher Child.*

George Stanley

When I First Met James

When I first met James, one of us was teaching at San Francisco State College – maybe we both were – I can't remember. It was 1968 or '9. James invited me to his birthday party, at his flat on Waller St. I was the first guest to arrive. James led me into the kitchen. On the kitchen table stood six bottles of Jack Daniels and six of Jameson. I said, "It will be a good party", and that's all I remember of it.

Jack Spicer died in 1965 and Patrick Kavanagh in 1967. So James and I found each other in San Francisco, bereft in a way, and made friends by introducing each other to them. Although, actually, it was that ruffian printer, Graham Mackintosh of White Rabbit Press, who did the introduction of James to Jack. But I've always said James and I exchanged masters.

I was at loose ends then, in that city, my home town, which was losing its soul. Progressive San Francisco, poetic San Francisco, Catholic San Francisco, all coming to an end. San Francisco would enter the demoralization of the 70s, from which it would emerge half theme park and half generic. I needed Kavanagh's poetry then, and James's early poetry too, for that rapt, devoted air of unconcern for whatever was not of the truth of the poem.

James gave me a fresh start in poetry; it was like one of those second acts Scott Fitzgerald said could never happen in American lives.

I remember another birthday party, this one in Coolgreany, Wexford, James's manse. I remember more than one. In the early 90s I used to hang out in Dublin, waiting to find out from Liam O'Connor when I could come to Coolgreany, when there'd be room, when all the students would have gone back to America, and I could come down on the train and spend long summer days with James and Jim and Liam – days of joy – for me, an Irish-American, riding around in the presence of the past – somehow elusively mine – to hotels and beaches and pubs.

And in James's kitchen there was the small eighteenth-century shot glass, out of which I would drink "wee goldies". This term, out of a Scottish detective novel, caused James great amusement. About ten p.m.

it would be time for drinks at Rafferty's – front room full of smoke – me holding two pints – nowhere to put either of them down, so drink them and then James says, "Another pint" – now that's not quite a question. No, I've had too many. "Glass", then. That definitely isn't a question. OK, glass. And then, glass, glass, glass. Then, of course, pint.

At that birthday party there was whiskey and ham and salads and rolls and I had brought little Canadian flags – I don't remember why – I think it was the time I had arrived from Moscow – I had meant to give them to children there. James placed them between the salads. Jim must have taken this photo, outside the house, in the back – but now I think this was a later birthday party – James is wearing mouse ears, Liam a black fedora, James's sister Nora is holding a cake, it looks like it's about to slip from her hands – I have a wreath on my head – the students are campy indolent Vikings or Teutonic knights.

Last time I saw James was in Dublin, but it was only a half-hour's audience – he was on his way to Spain. Next time I believe it will be in James's third Rome – Milwaukee – I hope very soon.

Happy Birthday, dear friend.

Love,

George

GEORGE STANLEY was born and raised in San Francisco. He was educated by the Jesuits in Bohemian (i.e., non-Mormon) Salt Lake City, and by Jack Spicer and Robert Duncan in North Beach. He taught English in colleges in British Columbia for many years, and now lives in Vancouver. His most recent book of poetry is *A Tall, Serious Girl* (Qua Books, 2003).

DANIEL TOBIN

Oscar Wilde in Racine (for James Liddy)

I picture you the image
of Speranza's bad boy,
exiled from the holy land
of *poesie pure*
who having mesmerized
the crowd in cowpoke saloons
arrived at the third coast
of this our middle west
to wow the dull heads
of a moralized majority.

It's a wonder the rabble
never ran him out of town,
back to the ruckus
of Salome's palace.
Yet, here, James, you found
your earthly paradise,
Milwaukee's Wilde-man,
your life – gout and all –
a light-footed bunbury
all the way from Coolgreany
to Kavanagh's Dublin,
from Ginsberg's teeming Haight
to River West barrooms
and the sexy East Side.

You'll hoist pints in heaven
with Baudelaire and Kerouac,
with Hartnett and Beckett
and Clare of Kilkee.
You'll officiate Lughnasa
with Spicer and Lorine,
and keep the *craic* going
in the next life after hours.

They're toasting you, James,
at Listwan's, The Shamrock,
at Annie's, The Landmark,
and Kit Nash's Bar,
roused in smoky Axel's
where time swims in neon,
all the young muses,
all the beautiful gathering.

DANIEL TOBIN is the author of three books of poems, *Where the World is Made*, co-winner of the 1998 Katherine Bakeless Nason Prize, *Double Life* (both Louisiana State University Press, 2004), and *The Narrows* (Four Way Books, 2005); as well as a book of criticism, *Passage to the Center: Imagination and the Sacred in the Poetry of Seamus Heaney* (University of Kentucky Press, 1998). His work has been anthologized in *The Bread Loaf Anthology of New American Poets*, *The Norton Introduction to Poetry*, *Hammer and Blaze* and elsewhere. He is presently Chair of the Department of Writing, Literature and Publishing at Emerson College in Boston.

Terence Winch

James Liddy: Real Ideas from Living

There is no turning in the widening gyre, no sailing to Byzantium (except by allusion), and no digging metaphors out of the Ulster bog. That's not what goes on in James Liddy's universe. Nor is the language he has invented a close relation to that of the stately anthology pieces of the Yeatsian-Heaneyan Irish mainstream. Liddy is cruising along in a very different vessel, one full of leaks and misdirection, but often making for a more exciting ride.

One reason for this is that James Liddy is the most American of Irish poets, his work clearly freed from worry about his place in the limited-membership ranks of the Irish Literary Establishment. There is a liberating, off-handed abandon to his poems, much more Whitman than W.B.Y. But he is also funny ("I Hear the Wife of the Governor of Wisconsin Singing") and in this way is more like the New York School (O'Hara, Ashbery, Ted Berrigan) than anything found in the self-mythologizing of Yeats, the sincere expansiveness of Whitman, or the authoritative meaningfulness of Heaney. In some ways, Liddy is a closer relative to Oscar Wilde ("I want to find the Wildeness of everything") and Allen Ginsberg ("Ginsberg bestowed liberation") than he is even to Jack Spicer or Paddy Kavanagh. Pleasure, most often an extract of sex or alcohol, is always near at hand in his poems. The language shortcuts to the action, whether sexual, aesthetic, or spiritual.

Many of his poems are letters to friends, as many of his letters to friends are poems. He can't seem to help himself:

> I am in the waves of drink and love and drowning:
> I wish the first stayed in the ocean the second in Ireland
> and the last in Arcadia. The last is driving me to the others,
> not for so long in my recorded history has this weary indoors heart been so massaged.
>
> [letter dated December 19, 1978]

> You'll be glad to know that my soul is being
> looked after. I have discovered a huge church, across
> the river, in a neighbourhood of small taverns and
> stores. It's Polish, it has Polish services, Polish
> confession. But every Saturday at 9:30 it has Latin

Mass. But there's always a problem for a Christian.
The Saturday bars close at 3:30 a.m. Not enough
Time for the Lord's grace to enter and settle in me.
After the soul the body.
[letter, March 1978]

"Or there is a poetry", Liddy writes in another letter ("Open Letter to the Young about Patrick Kavanagh"), "in which real ideas from living come at us. This kind can be a direct statement with a reference *behind* to the story of what happened to the poet. It relies on the mind staying alive, on the man making the statement keeping his emotional intelligence alive".

Direct but mysterious statements that seem to contain a world of reference behind them: this quality pervades *A Munster Song of Love and War*, the extraordinary chapbook published by White Rabbit in 1971. I came upon it in a bookstore in Boston in 1973 and was transfixed:

He'd be alive today if he wasn't pretty
He was gorgeous.
His beauty overcame his enemies and the
  enemies of Ireland
    and it was jealousy
    of his prettiness
    that has lain him
On the floor with his head open.
There are not enough mirrors in the bath
Rooms of Munster to shout how nice looking
  he was and awkward
  with a gun.

This was my first encounter with James's work, and I was deeply impressed that an Irish poet could be using language in such uninhibited, erotic, and anti-academic ways. Earlier, he had exhorted Irish poets to "park the paraphernalia out in the sunlight/Do not let it into the poem".

I also like that in Liddy's paraphernalia-free poems, "[t]he characters keep weeping to the accordion". "The accordion doesn't lie", we learn elsewhere. Finally, the box, that ascendant instrument in which so much Irish music finds surprising and subtle expression, has an advocate:

Praying that God becomes tender enough
to take up his gold squeeze box
and play a set with the new arrival
who has no need for purification

because tunes are receipts for existence
and an Irishman believes in anything
more than he believes in nothing.

James Liddy has accomplished what many only aspire to: he has created a remarkable language and voice unmistakably his own.

TERENCE WINCH recently published a book of non-fiction stories about his life in traditional Irish music called *That Special Place: New World Irish Stories* (Hanging Loose, 2004). He has also published three books of poems: *Irish Musicians/American Friends* (Coffee House Press, 1986), which won an American Book Award, *The Great Indoors* (Story Line Press, 1995), winner of The Columbia Book Award, and *The Drift of Things* (The Figures, 2001); and a book of short stories called *Contenders* (Story Line, 1989).

CHARLES BUKOWSKI

Letter to James Liddy

~~Los Angeles~~ Lost Angels
May 26, 1969

Hello James Liddy:

a house in Ireland? shit, you're really living! when do I get my piece of the cake?

o.k., thanks for BLUE HOUSE. but I thought I was the original beercan poet. you're even drinking my brand – Miller's. but no cigars – so I still hold a small edge.

will mail you a copy of LAUGH LITERARY #1, slow mail tomorrow, also NOTES OF A DIRTY OLD MAN – short stories, via Bukowski. let's hope it gets there before you make Ireland.

yes, the PENGUIN selection was <u>conservative</u>, and I tried to lay some of my later stuff on them, but no go. I've got another book coming up via ze Black Sparrow, couple of months, which I think will be the best. no title yet. but I am moving, as I am moving toward the grave, toward a poetry of explorative clarity – which really means writing about simple things in a profound and simple way and about profound things in a simple way, which really means just writing with clarity clarity clarity and avoiding all the horseshit poetic jingle traps. say ut like ya mean ut, dad. dirty stockings are closer to death than tombstones. so forth.

yes, sure, the poems you want to use, use them – you have my permission, all that technical bullshit. at least you choose poems nobody else chooses – they keep asking for OLD MAN, DEAD IN A ROOM and THE DAY I KICKED A BANKROLL OUT THE WINDOW. it makes me feel as if I'd only written two poems. I know there must be more because the typer ribbons keep wearing out.

of course, we're broke, so LAUGH LITERARY came out on a very limited budget – $80 for 500 copies – new photo process – off IBM, print really too small, and my young editor friend who I handed the copy over to seemed to have worked his whole family into the artwork, and it all came back a little corny, didn't match the cover, which I did, and which meant BLOOD, and here came all this carefully worked henshit around the good poems. a letdown, indeed, and I didn't say much to the kid – no use after the head is chopped off, but will have to watch him next time. I believe the poetic content to be superior, however, except my two poems, which the kid talked me into writing while I was drinking and talking to him. who's the god damned editor anyhow? anyhow, hope to go to larger format next time, 8 and one half by eleven, larger type, photos, poems, essays, screams ... besides attacking the dust-dry establishment poets ... establishment, that word's too easy, I'm getting tired of using it .... anyhow, would <u>also</u> like to attack the snobbery and pettishness and the publication of very bad work in the little magazines also – I really can't read the damn things, they're terribly weak, and careless and precious, and finally, juvenile and jerky. god, yes. so, anyhow, you've got a feel of what we need. we're not going to cause any literary revolution, but we hope to say a few things that haven't, for some reason, been said and to print the good clear strong poem – the poem that drinks beer and smokes cigars and laughs – sometimes. all right. but we have to reject almost everything and people get discouraged. we do too.

Jeffers preferred rocks; me too – I've never seen an
ugly one,

Buk

CHARLES BUKOWSKI (1920-1994), American novelist and poet, author of *Post Office*, *Factotum*, *Women*, *Ham on Rye*, *The Last Night of the Earth Poems* and numerous other books, all published by the Black Sparrow Press.

James Liddy

Her Disposition

I live in Yeats's old age
when my mother was young
and beautiful, an American
flapper in Dublin. Breathe
in foetus air of ignorance.

She took out her cigarette
on the edge of a great party,
she saw Yeats come down the stairs,
sat on the seat behind Lady Gregory,
I was like a snug inside her.

Joe McGrath the Sweepstake man
had taken her seat, he bought her
a box of chocolates and bowed.
At the interval Yeats stood
along the bar with arms folded,

people were afraid to go up
and talk to him. His gaze travelled
towards mother. She looked back
over her scotch thinking,
If I touch the hem of his shirt

I will be cured of my husband,
be released in my own beauty
on recognisance of my own desire,
I must be beautiful, pass on
that which becomes beautiful.

She stayed in the Firbolg village
Collected Poems on her table,
the doctor drove out to his patients
met her at night in the golf club,
she wept into my eyes.

previously unpublished

Una O'Higgins O'Malley

Restoration

So – is it all unravelling,
the ritual of book and candle,
of jewelled mitres and the golden staffs
of stern authority,
the labyrinths of polished corridors,
the swelling organs and the potted palms,
the whispered confidences
and the solemn portraits
done in oils to emphasise the ego?

Are we dealing with re-vision
in this new century?
The antique titles and the purple rings,
the convent parlours and the Confirmation banquets,
even the customary deferences – all are going,
disappearing back through time and time
from gold to brass to copper
and finally to carpenters' timber;
to the smooth carved wood of a shepherd's crook
and the cot of a simple manger,
to the savage strength of a criminal's cross
suspending in shame
our one necessity.

Are we tracing back and back to bread and wine
laid on a supper table,
to the problems of hungry lambs and sheep,
to the challenge of loving,
to an empty tomb laid bare
of the risen Saviour
and when we have got that far
will we then address His simple question
"Do you love me?"

I am from heads held high, stiff upper lips
and "the Clan's" affectionate laughter
where the pain was seldom spoken to the children
– and never among the teacups.

I am from Celtic spirals and the unresolved riddles
of twisted serpents scrolled on holy pages;
I am from dancing-class and make-believe
and graven plaque on cenotaph unheeded.

I am from motherhood and meetings
and an unrelenting trail of grocery trolleys;
I am from history and politics
and letters to the press and pictures of my father.

I am from lines of pilgrims thumbing beads upon their journeys,
from surgeon's spattered vests and the near-certainty of an all-loving
Godhead
I am from pardon and from protest – and like the spirals
I return to where I came from.

UNA O'HIGGINS O'MALLEY (1927-2005), daughter of Kevin O'Higgins, the assassinated Minister for Justice of the Irish Free State, was a well-known campaigner for political solutions to the Northern Troubles and was a co-founder of the Glencree Centre for Reconciliation. Her books are *From Pardon and Protest* (2001, memoir), *Twentieth Century Revisited* (2003, poems) and *Friends in High Places: Words of Inspiration* (2005), all published by Arlen House.

Kevin T. McEneaney

Hibernian Gold

One of the less obvious dialectics leveraging James Liddy's work is the tension of the domestic, both in his preoccupation with his parents and the exuberance of the same-sex intimacy he charts – the domestic remains within "the Kavanagh/Liddy notion of sincerity and self-revelation"[1] – yet I will suggest that the achievement refutes the premature and facile charge of *naïveté* Michael Smith here levelled against both Kavanagh and Liddy in a patronizing moment of cavalier dismissal. Never simple, Liddy's domestic hauntings exude gratitude and angst, acceptance and loss, ecstasy and alienation. How does Liddy manage to encompass such a range of drama within this most central theme?

The photograph, a central organizing device, presents what is there and what is not there. In "The Apparitions", from the collection *Gold Set Dancing*, we have the photo of the sixteen poets at Thor Ballylee, which includes Liddy, but the two most important Irish poets, Yeats and Kavanagh, are not there. Liddy meditates upon the ghostly presence of W.B. Yeats, but Patrick Kavanagh was "not invited, too dangerous, too tall".[2] The poem employs the image of gold to trace the genealogy of real poetry: the urbane poet Yeats writing about the countryside and able to churn "beautiful butter"; the rural poet Kavanagh moving to the city with the eloquence of his "golden rudeness"; then Liddy leaving Ireland for Wisconsin and the "gold of my own mind/and the half-bliss of ordinary life" (*GSD* 14). Some of the public may mistake poetry for the "official" photo, but poetry remains elsewhere, far from the expected in all of the examples cited – the locus of Liddy's poetry being neither city nor country, but his memories, especially of his parents, that ordinary which brings "surcease" (14). This poem is Liddy's central *apologia*, the key to his work, and the poem which decodes the book's title, the mind-memory dancing worthy of enduring. By the end of the poem the personal memory of his parents displace the career photo. Yet the pathos of the poem is about exile, exile from the Irish community of writers as well as the Ireland of his parents. Liddy's presence in the photo leads to a mind-meditation about absence and the absence of Patrick Kavanagh from the photo becomes symbolic of true poetry's plight and destiny – and in the same way Yeats resides as a ghostly presence not available to the senses.

Parental memories of the ordinary intrude, in rather startling quantity, throughout the course of Liddy's work. In "The Sound of a Moment at Scariff", it's "Mother and I in the/half stuffy kitchen/at Waterpark"[3] – an unlikely scenario for a poem that is a cosmic meditation on death, sex, and Brian Merriman. Such far-flung twinning is characteristic of Liddy's poetry, but the root of the ordinary holds it all together, "The acid leafstalks/of the common garden species" (*CP* 145). The people once at the party are now "ghosts/devouring my mental sights" (*CP* 144). But such memory-pictures of what once was, contrast vividly with the present, succouring "Peace, peaceful direction" (*CP* 146). The Proustian dialectic of the present and past in Liddy's work, or for that matter, Kavanagh's, provides a poetic chord or perhaps dissonant texture that echoes with genuine sentiment as any good poetry must, but never simplicity or an innocence that is ignorant.

In "Epithalamion", Liddy presents his marriage to poetry in two dimensions, the physical and the spiritual. The poem is divided into four parts: the first two parts are vision poems while the latter two are meditation poems. In Part I a sensual vision of youth finds its evocation ratified by the same-sex perceptions of Father Gerard Hopkins, S.J., whose own incomplete and failed "Epithalamion" for his brother Everard portrayed the idyllic union of boys bathing naked with water as an emblem of spousal love. Liddy's use of the word "Wedlock" (*CP* 169) is itself a direct quotation from Hopkins's "Epithalamion", but the meaning here is not romantically or Freudian symbolic, but sensually Incarnational: "Churchcock" – the sacred matter for both writers remains closeness with nature and sex, whether sublimated or indulged in. The elliptical dots Liddy employs here also allude to lost, destroyed, or censored lines of Hopkins' poem. Part II continues the theme of love's sensual river, this time ratified by Irish history and Blakean energy. Part III contemplates Church history, but veers off in another direction with personal talismans (blue stones) found on a beach, then the memory of two lovers by the statues of Goethe and Schiller at Washington Park – history as the personal inscription of love, then a deeper fall into meditation:

> Bliss lies in bed and looked down on us with mist eyes.
> "But you'll need a whole trousseau of graces." Stand up to this
> ordinary Bliss, be counted on Fr. Hopkins' gold breath. Be
> *numbered* in that cemetery. (Snow a star-hider and binder). (*CP* 176)

Sexual bliss may bring the union, but its endurance is tested by the ordinary. The comparison of ejaculation to snow emphasizes the transience of sexual satisfaction amid the length of commitment. The cemetery referred to might be the oblivion to which great poets are condemned to *in this lifetime* – as happened to Hopkins. The reference to Hopkins alludes to the struggle of the poet to wrestle with both the spiritual and the ordinary, as well as the need to turn both into poetry, even if that poetry be as ephemeral as snow, which is what writing poetry about the ordinary risks. Part IV of the poem meditates upon Liddy's parents, especially his mother, and the sexuality of the historical landscape in which the author was raised, conflating that landscape with the stem of his own sexuality until the concluding moral is attained:

> I think marriage is writing feminine, treasurable, untranslatable, letters like this. (*CP* 178)

Married to his art, his personality inscribes itself as male but the act of writing is the feminine wholeness to which he is committed. Yet there remains a level of his art that cannot be translated or corrupted by history – that secret level is the ordinary landscape of his family life and the self-confidence his parents gave him to embark upon his life-long commitment to poetry – the poem being ostensibly an epithalamion on his parents' wedding; yet the poem is a vision-meditation letter simultaneously to his male lovers and his parents, a celebration of his wedding to sensual life and the poetry that flows from it. Hopkins is Muse as well as saintly intercessor, just as in the Prologue ("lead us/like gospel daughters enchanted") to Daniel Berrigan's sequence "Homage to Gerard Manley Hopkins" (published in 1993, *after* Liddy's 1987 poem) where the fellow Jesuit likewise prays to saint Hopkins, as he employs the Jesuit method of meditation. Berrigan concludes his sequence with a Projectionist Credo of originality and incarnational mysticism:

> Gerard, I pray
> (your crown of thorns
> by Christ transfigured–
> laurel, aureole, leaf of gold)
>
> No base emulation
> mar my love![4]

But Liddy's most common Muse figures remain Kerouac, Kavanagh, Blake, Moore (George and Tom), Wilde – and his most constant – Jim Chapson, along with his most recent, Tom and Nora.

Jack Kerouac plays Muse for "Kerouac's Ronsard Dance", another major poem. The analogy between Kerouac and Ronsard rests upon parallels: just as Ronsard discarded the current medieval forms of poetry for Classical models, so Kerouac discarded contemporary models of poetry and prose – in poetry, the traditional English models for Chinese and Japanese models, while for prose he discarded the then-ossified American naturalism that reigned from Stephen Crane to Norman Mailer for a poetic prose rooted in the French Revolution and Rousseau, a more emotive prose that centred upon the punctuation of the people – the dash (and, of which, Wolfe Tone's prose was the uncontested master). A second parallel is Ronsard's revival of Anacreon, a celebration of life's brief pleasures of the moment, familiar to most English readers through Tom Moore's translations. The poem begins as a prayer to Our Lady that meditates on the deconstruction of Jesus, the historical Church, and Ronsard's presence at the royal court while weltering and swelling with extravagant Ronsard-like allegories that progress to the approval of Confession as a sacrament, and by implication the confessional poetic tradition of Wordsworth, Yeats, and Kavanagh. This leads to the celebration of the French Revolution ("a Republic of Stars") and the joke that "the Gallic Muses are transformed bag-ladies". All finds culmination in a solipsistic deconstructionist apotheosis of fervent delusion: "Jesus, Ronsard, Jack, I have become". Prayer has turned to mysticism, just as academic discourse has been displaced with a personal poetic: "Ronsard, c'est moi!" Echoing Flaubert on the character Emma Bovary, Liddy arrives at the realization that poetry lives in what he writes, not in the reconstructed fantasy of the academic world or in fantasies of other writers – that is his "awakening", the "process that blesses non-process" (*CP* 230).

The metaphor of dance that Liddy employs provides a declaration about his postmodernist technique, which communicates the intimacy and improvisation of dance – something different from both traditional English prosody and American Projectionist verse, a line with turns and veers with the energy of dance, but without obvious formalism. Liddy's near-Sufi dance theme presents a Christian incarnational aesthetic: "The dancer coaxing God out of his body to be". Such inclusive Taoism finds its parallel with one of Jack Kerouac's lesser-appreciated gems, *Satori in*

Paris (1966). Liddy's meditative use of deconstructionist motifs proffers parody of the academy, as he offers homage to Kerouac, and like Kerouac finds illumination in the ordinary present of his own life: "Glass,/condom, night-prowl, sunrise, take you all" (*CP* 230). Displacing the poem's amusing cerebral pyrotechnics, it discovers itself as an ode (one of Ronsard's favourite forms) to the ordinary, those "Cana moments" (*CP* 228) in which poetry transubstantiates the ordinary, the Eucharistic cinema theme of "Strawberries and Chocolate" (*GSD* 67-68).

Lest readers think that the contemporary French way is the route to travel, Liddy pointedly disabuses readers of that notion in "A Letter to Eamonn Wall" where instructional advice predominates: "Take long paragraph journeys but never turn them into/a text to please the French" (*CP* 277). The poem begins with an allusion to James Joyce's "Ivy Day in the Committee Room" from *Dubliners* (1914). The young poet is seriously advised to pray to Kerouac and Proust because of their originality, yet the central problem is how to be satiric ("mix in a little scorn") as one combines parody with a love that illuminates the ordinary. The preferred model is Joyce rather than Yeats: "The Avondale leaf lit Paris", being a reference to Joyce, the exiled leaf of Parnell. Similar advice can also be found in Thomas Moore's 1841 correspondence where he speaks of the "unembittered spirit, the ... freedom from all real malice with which, in most instances, this sort of squib-warfare has been waged by me".[5] As such, Liddy's advice remains a disclosure of his own Joycean methodology, if such a phrase can do justice to Liddy's seemingly improvisational style. Of course, it *was* Joyce who designed many of the concepts and parameters of the new *philosophes*, but the advice is to imitate the original not his knock-offs. One could argue that Joyce is the dominant French poet of the twentieth century, the prose poet after Chateaubriand whom French poets have been unable to displace. (Paul Eluard was smart to ignore Joyce as much as possible, and Tristan Tzara's late flowering in *Frère bois* stands as a near-enigmatic triumph). Joyce as mentor also appears on the cover of Liddy's *Comyn's Lay* (1978) with Liddy and Jim Chapson flanking the awkwardly cross-legged statue of Joyce in Zurich, which gauntly gazes into the mysterious beyond with Jimmy's F-finger prominently following his gaze. (*Chamber Pot Music* includes a poem on the photo, and one poem contains the brash and somewhat supercilious boast, "I adapt from Joyce".[6])

In "A Vision for the Visions of Kinsella", Liddy evokes the notorious anecdote about James Joyce crossing the Swiss border during World War

II – when his initial application was rejected for being a Jew, Joyce replied, "C'est le bouquet, vraiment".[7] In Liddy's poem, which meditates upon the fate of the great *sean nós* singer Joe Heaney (whose voice seemed to extend into the sunset rays when I heard him sing by the Hudson River in Croton, N.Y.) and a small circle of Irish friends exiled to American professorships, the central metaphor is the outer envelope of exile that cloaks the inner poetic-songster: the moral being that some form of exile is an advantage: "Be a Jew from the point of view/of experience".[8] And in "A Keening", Liddy exhorts, "May the hometown soil never lie on you" (*GSD* 11).

The theme of exile was central to Joyce and an important theme in Liddy's work; Liddy makes this theme a preoccupation in *Baudelaire's Bar Flowers* (1975), the most successful sequence he ever wrote – Liddy's contribution to the epyllion genre that so obsessed and inspired Ireland after Patrick Kavanagh's *The Great Hunger* (1942), generating Austin Clarke's *Mnemosyne Lay in Dust* (1966), Richard Murphy's *Battle of Aughrim* (1968), John Montague's *The Rough Field* (1972), Thomas Kinsella's *Butcher's Dozen* (1972), Brendan Kennelly's *Cromwell* (1983), Seamus Heaney's *Station Island* (1984), Desmond Egan's *Peninsula* (1992), James Simmons' *The Franconia Sequence* (1999), and Martin Mooney's *Grub* (2002).

The best of *Baudelaire's Bar Flowers* – prophesied by Knute Skinner's 1966 poem about Liddy "exiled" in Spain: "Pray for us, James; write us/a poem of such dimension"[9] – was in a form that Skinner used to write about Liddy – the letter poem. Six prose-letter poems are addressed to Paddy Kavanagh, while two verse-poems find address to Sainte-Beuve and Arthur Symons who "took photographs of thirty/of the houses he [Baudelaire] wept in".[10] Kavanagh appears as the saintly mentor who introduced Liddy to the artistic underworld: "If our country is Poetry then the name of the universe is Bohemia" (*BBF* 12). The second letter reveals that the whole book is both atonement and memorial to Kavanagh because shortly before his death Kavanagh was reading Baudelaire and wanted to discuss him, while Liddy preferred to listen to radio debate about gun-running; Kavanagh is the bridge to the Otherworld of poetry (*BBF* 16). The third letter praises Kavanagh and Baudelaire for rejecting academic claptrap and transcending worldly reality (*BBF* 23). The fourth letter finds correspondence between Baudelaire and Kavanagh on the matter of sex, agreeing with Yeats's critique of Ezra Pound's style as "sexless" (*BBF* 28). In the next letter homosexuality opens the door to poetic perception, just as it did for the two "immolated heterosexuals" (*BBF* 39). The last letter is both apotheosis and memorial to the poet of McDaid's (*BBF* 47) – a sincere and moving love letter to the dead poet. The point of this brief and somewhat superficial summary is that these letters are at the heart of the book as sequence – its genesis, its world of correspondences, the locus of inspiration and improvisation as well as intimate lament for a lost teacher and friend. During the course of the meditation academic ideas find presentation as seductive temptations, even possible maps, to be examined and rejected since their sterility cannot engender the world of poetic correspondences located in the bohemian world of love.

Liddy's subsequent sequence, *Corca Bascinn* (1977), employs the notion of exile in its concluding section – exile not so much from Ireland as from past lovers. Beginning with the desire to conjure an Irish Otherworld, the sequence resigns itself to the project of love in daily life amid the frontiers of not having a country, the Atlantic Ocean becoming the symbol of love.[11] Brian Arkins identifies the style of the book as "that of Joyce's interior monologue – as in Stephen Dedalus's musings on Sandymount Strand".[12] The concluding ninth section, labelled EXILE, begins: "I write June innerred petalled/Hibiscus letter to ex-lovers" (*CB* 59). Love imposes the memory-wound that afflicted Joyce and launches Liddy into "Mnemosyne's town" (*CB* 64) with the lyrical evocation of "Pollen-odoured warm warmer nights" (*CB* 59). Whatever the merits of the loose sequence as a unity, the poem "Proverbs of Corca Bascinn" still stands as an amusing and memorable masterpiece of a poet who has arrived at a significant synthesis, giving hints of the important work yet to come. One of my favourite lines in the poem: "The poet knows he is good when they say he cannot write verse" (*CB* 53). Like W.B. Yeats, much of James Liddy's achievement arrives in an autumnal breeze as it conjures the visceral romances of spring.

A significant aspect of the domestic in James Liddy's work moves in two directions: the many poems memorializing his mother Clare, and the threesome. The title poem of *Gold Set Dancing* presents the fantasy of the poet's mouth bestowing gold:

> take the dancers' hands and kiss them
> their ringed fingers turn to gold. (53)

With his Midas touch, the poet finds himself dancing with Nora and Tom, and this set, this threesome, becomes the image of ideal love, the golden dance. The author is in love with Tom, "a man who's just married". The eloquent poems that follow celebrate this dance. "Tom and Nora" portrays the passion and romanticism of the adoring outsider hosting his American visitors upon whom he keeps vigil. A second poem entitled "Gold Set Dancing" appears, a short prothalamion that acceptingly declares: "I'm in love with him [Tom] anyway/and will shine so" (*GSD* 56). Then the long *paean* for the newly married honeymooners in Venice ends with the word "feet" – so as to conjure the image of dance and capture the pathos of the temporarily exiled third lover whose feet lay planted on a different continent as his words dance for them.

The ardent romance of the threesome as the gold standard was the Beat ideal, both in life and fiction. Carolyn Cassady chronicled the threesome between her, her husband Neal Cassady, and Jack Kerouac, in her autobiography *Heart Beat* (1976), while Diane di Prima portrayed the pleasures of a fantasy threesome – herself, and the figures of Kerouac and Ginsberg – in *Memoirs of a Beatnik* (1969), which was a direct broadside aimed at merely monogamous relations: "The real horror, the real nightmare in which most of us are spending our adult lives, is the deep-rooted insidious belief in the one-to-one world".[13] Perhaps more significantly, the recent publication of Kerouac's novella *Orpheus Emerged* (2000) chronicles the antics of several college students. The would-be poet Michael and sardonic Paul (the Kerouac figure) possess a deep secret from which other friends are excluded. At school their friendship is strained by Michael's bad poetry and his immersion into two sordid affairs as he searches for a Muse he can't reduplicate. Kerouac's novella is a very early work written in the realistic-yet-romantic style of Willa Cather who, in *My Ántonia* (1918), briefly depicted a sexual foursome;[14] the name Paul in Kerouac's novella refers – by way of inscribing a modern bohemian version that updates Cather – to the short story "Paul's Case"; the plot has a happy ending when Helen, the beautiful Muse of both Paul and Michael, arrives on campus. Michael remains hysterical and suicidal but melts in her arms, unable to believe that she has come for *him* as well as Paul. The book concludes: "the miracle of wholeness was renewed".[15] Through the healing power of the threesome, Michael's potency as a poet is restored and he emerges reborn as Orpheus, an Orpheus who was dead as long as he looked back and lamented the loss of the loving trio, but now alive in the loving threesome united once more. For many of the so-called Beats the source of real poetry was conceived of as the trio, or some relationship like miscegenation outside conventional sociology. As

Carolyn Cassady said at a 1996 San Francisco symposium, speaking of her relationship with Neal Cassady and Jack Kerouac, "I had the best of all worlds – two men I really liked".[16]

The circumstances of Liddy's version of the threesome might be considered more romantic than Kerouac's version because it is more fully lived and tested – as the climax to *Gold Set Dancing*, bohemian romance persists into old age. Liddy's version is a mature book-end to Kerouac's libido-releasing and rather accomplished *bildungsroman*. In Liddy's sequence the wholeness emerges because he is both "woman and man" (*GSD* 52) through the writing of his poetry for the married couple, writing being the feminine act described in "Epithalamion".

While rigid moralists may scorn or deprecate the intimate loving triangle, the theme endures as one of the most difficult to paint without descending into propaganda or plain corny fluff. Ivan Turgenev lived that triangle and it remains the subtle and unstated fantasy of his masterful psychological study, the play *A Month in the Country* (1872). William Faulkner triumphed with the theme in *Pylon* (1935), while Ernest Hemingway failed with *Garden of Eden* (1986), as did Hollywood with the sentimental postcard of *Summer Lovers* (1982), set on the Greek island of Santorini. Popular culture has recently churned out entries like the superficial *Three of Hearts* (1993) and the more considerable improvisation of *Two Girls and a Guy* (1998), but they do not measure up to the marvellous romance of Catherine and her lovers cavorting on the Left Bank in Francois Truffaut's *Jules and Jim* (1962), although *Henry and June* (1990) captures fairly well much of the atmosphere of Henry Miller's and Anaïs Nin's obsessive writings. And yet none of this material can be situated in the hipster spirit-prayer of Liddy's "Buy a cinema ticket in memory" (*GSD* 68). That exile Havana prayer about a time when same-sex relations were tolerated in Cuba appears more akin to the spontaneous prayers of Ray Smith in *The Dharma Bums* (1958): "Thank you O Lord for returning my zest for life, for Thy ever-recurring forms in Thy Womb of Exuberant Fertility".[17] According to both Kerouac and Liddy, that zest, exuberance and fertility can't be found in a madhouse popular culture that is "supervised" (Kerouac, *DB*, 121) whether by consumer-obsessed moving images or sexual bigotry.

While the literary treatment of the threesome is as old as the Bible (Jacob, Leah, and Rachael), the honest success of Liddy's "vigil" treatment of his relationship with Tom and Nora brings high romance to a difficult genre: "O Bridge of Sighs where lovers desperately found their rosary beads" (*GSD* 57). When combined with wit, sincerity can succeed in communicating an earned pathos and such intimate recordings of emotion endure as some of the American Beats' finest works. Yet the question remains: is Ireland comfortable with the thought that it has produced one of the most eloquent of Beat poets? Can it rejoice in that admission?

A word about Liddy's use of the word "gold", a motif that threads its way through the poems of *Gold Set Dancing*. In this book the word consistently refers to what is lasting, to those memory-pictures that continue the lively dance of dialogue with the present and which contain a spiritual energy. At the climactic ending of Kerouac's *On the Road* (1957), Sal Paradise, the Kerouac-narrator, has a primal Christian vision, much like the Resurrection-vision that changed the life of the apostle Paul. Dean Moriarty and Sal are in Mexico where they experience a hellish night of swarming insects, then a Malcolm Lowry-like dream of a white horse (referring to the concluding mystic vision of *Under the Volcano*). But in the dawn desert Sal spots the shepherds, "dressed as in the first times". Sal yells to Dean to wake up and see this, for it is no dream: "wake up and see the golden world that Jesus came from".[18] Kerouac's visionary climax brings the narrative "to the end of the road" with the sense that the characters have finally achieved the apotheosis of their quest, finding rebirth in this golden light. Likewise Liddy employs the word "gold" in this questing visionary sense in the poem "Gold Set Dancing":

> the gold of Ireland did seduce
> then I arrived in gold rush
> town San Francisco;
> I replaced home mind,
> emigrated to god and play. (52)

Gold represents both bohemian quest and achievement, as well as the ring of commitment to unconventional love.

Liddy's poetry has a density and the dance-set texture of complexity blessed with a sophisticated humour that may at times discourage the breezy reader and, in this respect, Liddy holds up a mocking mirror to the self-conscious Academe of the latter twentieth century. The question whether Liddy's Blakean or Baudelairean sexuality is rooted in the New Testament, or Joyce, or Freud, proffers little to contemplate, yet it provides some of his most exalted poetry. His best poetry dwells in personal vision, rooted in Yeats, Kavanagh, and Kerouac, especially the Kerouac of *The Dharma Bums*, although Liddy never embraced Buddhism and has retained a clear-eyed Christianity with many of his poems echoing Church litany. Rummaging through the rucksack of his emotions, both his wanderings and family portraits, he presents an anti-bourgeois critique of his contemporary world. The personal and the intellectual appear as a seamless robe wherein the intellectual supports emotions caught in the moment or in memory. Although there are several deep intellectual influences on Liddy's work, his poetry exudes the unpredictable energy of the "sidereal hatchery". The cosmic libido of Liddy's poetry also discovers a dialectical romanticism wherein life's greatest loves include those exiled, platonic romances which elude our more ordinary embrace: "Mates you didn't hutch".[19]

NOTES

[1] Michael Smith, "The Contemporary Situation in Irish Poetry", in Douglas Dunn, ed., *Two Decades of Irish Writing* (Cheadle: Carcanet Press, 1975), 161.

[2] James Liddy, *Gold Set Dancing* (Cliffs of Moher: Salmon Publishing, 2000), 14. Future references to this work will be noted in parentheses in the text.

[3] Liddy, *Collected Poems* (Omaha: Creighton University Press, 1994), 143. Future references to this work will also be noted in parentheses in the text.

[4] Daniel Berrigan, *And the Risen Bread: Selected Poems, 1957-97* (New York: Fordham University Press, 1998), 328.

[5] Howard Mumford Jones, *The Harp That Once: Tom Moore and the Regency Period* (New York: Henry Holt and Company, 1937), 194-95.

[6] Liddy, *Chamber Pot Music* (Berkeley: hit & run press, 1982), 14

[7] Richard Ellmann, *James Joyce: New and Revised Edition* (Oxford: Oxford University Press, 1982), 736.

[8] Liddy, *A White Thought in a White Shade* (Dublin: Kerr's Pinks, 1987), 47.

[9] Knute Skinner, *The Cold Irish Earth: New and Selected Poems of Ireland, 1965-1995* (Cliffs of Moher: Salmon Publishing, 1996), 69.

[10] Liddy, *Baudelaire's Bar Flowers* (Santa Barbara: Capra Press, 1975), 51. Future references to this work will be noted in parentheses in the text.

[11] Liddy, *Corca Bascinn* (Dublin: The Dolmen Press, 1977), 59. Future references to this work will also be noted in parentheses in the text.

[12] Brian Arkins, *James Liddy: A Critical Study* (Galway: Arlen House, 2001), 22.

[13] Diane di Prima, *Memoirs of a Beatnik* (New York: Olympia Press, 1969), 103-04.

[14] Willa Cather, *My Ántonia* (New York: Signet, 1994), 233.

[15] Jack Kerouac, *Orpheus Emerged* (New York: ibooks, 2000), 147.

[16] Ann Charters, *Beat Down to Your Soul* (New York: Penguin, 2001), 630.

[17] Kerouac, *The Dharma Bums* (New York: Viking, 1958), 126.

[18] Kerouac, *On the Road* (New York: Viking, 1957), 299.

[19] Liddy, *Moon and Star Moments* (New York: At-Swim Press, 1982).

KEVIN T. MCENEANEY

Quick Sketch of the Bishop before Beatification

Wexford acorns weep diamonds
as the brown bull contemplates
the cavorting of hybrid grasshoppers.
This occurred on our watch
when the sky turned chartreuse
as meteors fell bouncing like hailstones
and cats mewed on banisters.

Back at the rectory with mouldy walls
he chanted of the old days
when lilies owned the fields
and the pubescent reality
of a used-car dealer
working in a world-wide discount chain
was still a milk-cow fantasy.

Chaplets of bridal wreaths
around the neck of the next
generation bowing to their penance
of spontaneous cloud writing.

The Jovial wink and sputter
that made the night glitter
with a whisper of whiskey
and the relevance of what
could not be remembered.

A poet who never lost his sense of humour?
Sometimes it happens
when the road remains enshrouded in fog.

Something of a Joycean inscape
in the way he moved inside the corrugated landscape
and maybe people dreaming.
And for that few forgave,
yet he took up his green crosier laughing
as the sunset filled his mouth
with a golden glow,
speaking quietly of butterflies
spotted and bent dizzy
over the scent of a lily.

KEVIN T. MCENEANEY is the author of numerous book reviews and over forty articles. His chief books are *Longing* (1997), the Buddhist sequence *The Enclosed Garden* (1990) and the yet-to-be published epyllion *Admundo*.

THOMAS MCGONIGLE

Knowing a Writer

JAMES LIDDY – one among – ruined my life. In the spring of 1965, when I was twenty, he paid me four guineas for what became my first published poem.

SHORT THOUGHT ON DEATH
Bright white bird
come
claim me
for black paradise.

I had to spend one of those guineas on a round of drink in O'Dwyer's on Leeson Street. The poem appeared in the final issue of *Arena*, the most important little magazine to appear in Dublin in the 60s, which Liddy founded, edited and funded.

I had crossed the invisible line and now 40 years later what is there to show for it?

James Liddy published his one absolutely essential book, *Baudelaire's Bar Flowers*, in 1975 with White Rabbit Press in California. A mixing of prose, poetry and translation, it is unique in Irish literature for its daring, frankness and isolating eccentricity. All the wastes of Dublin life are contained within its 53 pages: alcoholism, convoluted homosexuality, and the sour smell of suicide.

I have known James Liddy for more than half of my life and have known him for more than half of his life, a life of great inherited wealth (for Ireland), a life in which he has never had to work at anything he did not want to do, a life given over to poetry but not doomed by it – a well furnished bohemian life.

I used to visit him in Milwaukee in the early 80s and would sit with him in the various bars where he presided surrounded by his "angels", Catholic boys of a confused sexuality, and he listened much as Warhol would do in New York and he prospered within his surroundings. Things changed when the cannibal Dahmer stalked the bars and James Liddy rose in the university.

However, sitting one evening in Axel's Tavern with James and Father Crewe, a local parish priest, and the conversation turns to a discussion of the changes in the Catholic Church. It is mentioned that the Sacrament of Penance is now called the Sacrament of Reconciliation, and now for confession you sit at a table across from a priest and discuss your failings or problems. James protests:

> "I cannot accept it. Confession must be the going into a dark cabinet and getting down on the knees".

Father Crewe says:

> "Oh James, the reason you have to go to confession is that you were on your knees".

Sadly, James Liddy gave his life over to the meanness of being a tenured professor and never invited me to sup at his university for even one visit – you were waiting for the resentment, I trust? I, who had published him at length in *Adrift*, I, who had invited him to read both in New York and even in, of all places, Milwaukee. He did publish me in his throwaway magazine *The Gorey Detail*, which as far as I know was read by no one, a product of the arts gravy-train of the New Ireland.

James Liddy, may he live long in the final hope of Purgatory, as Julian Green told me was his only hope in his 94th year. I think of all the dead who, when living, James brought me in contact with, Brian Higgins, the flagrant saint John Jordan, Edward Dahlberg, Eugene Lambe, Francis Stuart, Liam O'Flaherty, Jim Fitzgerald, Michael Hartnett, Richard Riordan, Fintan the Taxidriver, Patrick Kavanagh, and those close now to death, Anthony Cronin, Leland Bardwell, Philip Hobsbaum, Ben Kiely, Teresa Nolan ...

Of course the past is dead and waits for ... but, please, not the damp trap of nostalgia ... today we are upright waiting.

In James Liddy's apartment back then in Milwaukee there would be of course many books in bookcases and then books resting against the wall about the edge of the sitting room floor, upright with their covers to the view. There would be books on the top edge of the sofa and as you sat they might tip over into your lap. James Liddy does not watch television, go to the movies or listen to music. He does listen to words on the radio. We have shared a reading of Jack Kerouac, Jack Spicer, and John Wieners. He told me of observing so long ago Denis Donoghue

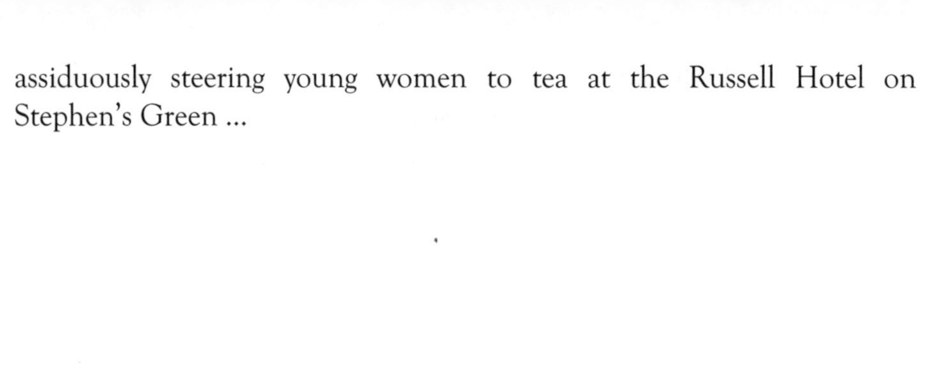

assiduously steering young women to tea at the Russell Hotel on Stephen's Green ...

THOMAS MCGONIGLE has published two novels, *The Corpse Dream of N. Petkov* (Dalkey Archive Press and Northwestern University Press) and *Going to Patchogue* (Dalkey Archive Press). He was the editor of *Adrift*, a magazine of Irish and Irish-American writing. He writes now for *The Los Angeles Times*, *Bookforum*, *The Washington Post* and *The Guardian* (London), and has of late taught at NYU, Rutgers, and John Jay College of Criminal Justice, CUNY.

James Liddy

Correspondences

Whatever it is it is the murmur of evil
It comes on like a soldier in a bar
Hearts are not had hearts are found
And you are chosen for the works of love.

It is not the love college kids pretend
It is not the brotherhood of soldiers it is soldiers
It was always this black mystery
Of you and a few others being chosen.

The beauty demons bring does not dry up
In fervid hearts of perverts lies The Church Daemoniacal
The opposite of wives the murmur of evil
The soldiers soldiers coming on.

from *Baudelaire's Bar Flowers* (1975)

JOHN LIDDY

Making Up

I once wrote a poem for my cousin James called "Instead of Clocks". It refers to moments and events, family and places, and its overall intention was to express a will to sustain a friendship that had temporarily gone off course. The poem ends with the lines:

> Pints pulled in Collins' with no less
> A love than one hand round the glass
> Where another hand had been.

I was the barman and James the customer, and the glass, I suppose, a symbol of that bond I did not want to see broken, one we have been fortunate to enjoy, uninterrupted but for that brief lapse, since those Limerick days in the 70s. The poem now speaks to me of how poets make-up in poems, how blood is thicker than Guinness!

And that is what James has been doing all his life. Making-up in poems. There is no real falling out amongst friends. And he is a great friend to have. Book after book pushes the horizon of the poem tantalisingly out-of-reach, yet keeping it within the receptive reader's grasp. Their central themes of family, friends, love, sex, Irish politics, Catholicism and his own Liddyesque brand of humour and fun may madden the more serious minded and delight the more rebellious. I remember being shocked out of my Limerick doldrums by poems such as "Personal Odyssey" (*In a Blue Smoke*), the Spanish influences I was later to come to in "The Republic 1939" (*Blue Mountain*), the politics of our own divided family history mirrored in *A Munster Song of Love and War* and the most original treatment of County Clare I have ever read in *Corca Bascinn*. Later, I was to steal moments of sheer awe on reading the unrivalled, unequalled mastery of *Baudelaire's Bar Flowers* and that confessional mix of life's emotions in *A White Thought in a White Shade*. All of these books and more have allowed me to look into the heart of my cousin, our shared family cupboard, and see with clearer vision my own path.

James has always accompanied me on my very different journey because, perhaps, we share that passion for the poem. He has taught me to smile wryly at my most serious subjects and see how the other branches of the same tree can cast similar shadows. *Trees Warmer than Green* and *She Is Far from the Land* are two such teacher-troves I go back to again and again.

There are, of course, other poems and books that I could mention but I didn't set out to write about the work. What I intended to say was *go sona an lá a rugadh é* and that when we meet in Limerick or Madrid, Dublin or Wexford Town, the clock will stop as we slip into family history or plot a poetic collaboration. We will glint over the rims of our raised glasses and drink to cousinly friendship and to many more *feliz cumpleaños.*

Madrid, May 22, 2004

JOHN LIDDY

Instead of Clocks (for cousin James)

The brush of bush along the local road.
Moments of pure repose in the cool
sunwindow of encyclical poetry,
recalling times when we sprinted
for the train to El Escorial,
you preferring to pray outside
not genuflect within the cold
austerity of Philip's citadel.
A white thought behind the mask
mischievous. Nimble.

The house in Kilkee with your mother
reaching down the ladder of paperbacks,
graciously sharing her bottle of tolerance.
The kitchen humming a pretence of grief
from the lips of your radio days,
a thousand cups of kind Josie's kitchen tea.

Bird swallowed poetry evening
in the garrison castle.
Was there a hack amongst us that night?
The Sarsfield in its cosy tomb,
our fathers remembered in the antique
bar dust of Charlie St. George:
a shrivelled rugby ball,
the burnt keys of the piano.

Elsewhere in the reflection of sea-lakes,
in the white of a handkerchief
plucked from a Leeson Street flat,
In the vales of the fallen –
mouths groping for lips on Reeves' path,

pints pulled in Collins' with no less
a love than one hand round the glass
where another hand had been.

(This is a revised version of a poem which appeared in Wine and Hope, *1999)*

JOHN LIDDY's poetry collections include *Boundaries* (1974), *The Angling Cot* (1991), *Song of the Empty Cage* (1996), *Wine and Hope/Vino y Esperanza* (1999) and *Cast-A-Net/Almadraba* (2003). He is based in Spain and currently working on a volume of new and selected poems.

Dermot Bolger

At Twenty

She said, "I'm suffering from the most terrible flu,
If we sleep together I'll pass it on to you".

He lay in bed for four days after she left,
Shivering and waking up drenched in sweat,
His throat raw, legs unable to take his weight:
He paid this price happily, with no regret.

Dermot Bolger was born in Dublin in 1959. His nine novels include *The Journey Home*, *The Valparaiso Voyage* and the recently acclaimed *The Family on Paradise Pier*. His debut play, *The Lament for Arthur Cleary*, received The Samuel Beckett Award; *From These Green Heights* won the Irish Times/ESB Award for Best New Irish Play of 2004. He is author of seven volumes of poetry. Bolger has championed new Irish writers, firstly through Raven Arts Press, and later as co-founder of New Island Books. He devised the best-selling collaborative novels, *Finbar's Hotel* and *Ladies Night at Finbar's Hotel*, and edited *The Picador Book of Contemporary Irish Fiction*.

GABRIEL ROSENSTOCK

Bladhmann

Bladhmann was a busybody, a boaster, a braggart, a boozer, a bamboozler, a blackguard and a proper bastard to boot. Found in a basket, he boasted blue blood and black pudding. A belligerent babbler, a bucko, he had no more sense than a blundering baboon that had lost its bearings below in the boggy backwoods. Addicted to bilberries, bacon and beet-root, all boiled in a bubbling blend of buttermilk and beestings over a bonfire of bog-oak, with a hint of basil, he claimed it was brilliant for biliousness – but all he got from it was botulism.

A biased backscratcher, a bogtrotter and a blithering bigamist from the back of beyond, he bullied and head-butted his way through the bowers of boredom, balking at bloody well nothing. To those who couldn't be bothered with his brash, bestial ways he would blurt: "Bah!" or "Boo!" or "Bitch" or "Bollocks". Nothing was beneath the boor. He had a bandicoot's bladder for brains and was as bald as a banana. He was what you might call a bit of a *breallsún* or even a *bromán*.

A busker, he had his own bohemian bodhrán band – a blot on the face of Banba – a band that bellowed baffling, bawdy ballads interspersed with blarney. The lyrics were banal bacchanalia: indeed, such barbarous baloney was never broadcast, before or since:

Bend an ear to the bleary banshee
Is she bawlin' for you, Bill, or me?
Is it my bones she's blashtin' – or yours?
Sure them banshees are blisterin' oul' hoors.

And if this wasn't bad enough, sporting a bright-blue bandana, Bladhmann butchered the bagpipes as well – blessed sight to behold – at a pitch he claimed would blight all bacteria. When they forgot the words, these bulky boyos would do a belly dance in their bermudas and hob-nailed boots while squeezing the bejaysus out of the blackheads on their bulbous noses and knocking down the bloody marys like billyo.

Bladhmann was the bane of Baile Átha Cliath in those bygone, blundering days and many a brave attempt was made by barrister, bard, bureaucrat, bailiff, bystander and *brúisc* to find a loophole in Brehon Law whereby he could be banished – but he remained the bigoted barnacle he was from birth. Bliss was it for him to burst blithely into a barber-shop – not for back and sides for he was bald, but to bark his bawdy lyrics and have himself a bit of a brawl or a brouhaha. In an attempt to boost his battered career, he would barge and bludgeon his way into barn-dance, bingo or bar mitzvah ... no beach party or game of bridge was safe as he bored his way through bouncers like a bungee-jumping billy goat gone berserk in a blizzard. No barrier, bulwark or boulder could resist this ballistic boomerang. Two bonny bats bedded down beautifully in his belfry and a queen bee made bedlam in his bonnet.

The bare fact that he never took a bath (except in his own bile) never bothered him as he believed that the brazen sun beamed bravely from his bountifully bearded bottom. The brunt of the matter is that Bladhmann was a beast and a bosthoon, a bit of a *buaiciollach*: britches half down, he would befriend buxom, blushing beauties in the local bordello with such besotted, boisterous balderdash as: "Bless you, Biddy, my brunette, I bet you've a bonny beaver I could bung before breakfast". Who'd bed Bladhmann? The biddies gave him a wide berth or blithely stomped on his bunions, saying: "Begorrah that's a bad dose of the B.O. you have there, you *bodach*!" He would take this beneficence blandly, brace his big biceps or bare buttocks and, bright as a button, though beetle-browed, engage in a little pocket billiards and belch briskly (in Belgian).

He collected bikinis and brassieres and bonked them beamishly on bleak brillig mornings in his beehive hut, thereafter bestowing on them the bonus of his bloated bladder and bowels, blaspheming all the while, his baleful bloodshot eyes becoming blank. The ensuing blackout was his only form of bodily bliss, or the brink thereof.

He kept a burping budgerigar – booty it was, but no beauty – in a brimming bucket and fed it on bed-bugs, biscuit-beetles, baked bluebottles, barbecued burgoo and all sorts of brock. He became a blasted burden to himself once he lost the budding bloom of youth and, to belittle his barren sorrow, he acquired the bold habit of putting a bleached finger up his buttered, burning bum and other such barmy acts of buffoonery which only lead to *buinneach* which, as everyone knows, could mean anything, i.e. a discharge, blotches and sores, corns, diarrhoea, rapid blinking, scour, blisters, blah-bloody-blah.

When Bladhmann got over the *buinneach* anyway – whatever it be let it be – he tried body building. One morning, beholding his bronzed body in the mirror, he bawled "Blimey!" complaining that his late spring "no bud or blossom showeth". His agony was brutal, bitter, his self-pity boundless. It broke what little heart was in his bosom when his beloved budgie burped his last burp, banjaxed by bubonic plague. Out of the blue he sent for Burton, a brilliant bishop (*beatae memoriae*), known for his bulldozing banter, a bony, balanced, bilingual bisexual whom he, Bladhmann, first badgered and then buggered over brunch, without as much as a *buon giorno* exchanged between them, both of them bristling with briny rage. Such bobbery! The bishop buzzed in his burgundy and burst a blood vessel. A bracing experience it was not and Bladhmann brooded about his bungling for the best part of Bealtaine.

His breath stank from here to Borneo, billowing through the biosphere to the extent that birds, especially buntings, bypassed his abode and one broken barnacle goose fell like a bomb to earth, beheading itself. He decided to brush up, to clean out his bowels once and for all by consuming borax mixed with battered bran and beeswax. A brain-boggling experience. He felt boxed in, bitten, benumbed, betrayed, banjaxed. He took to the brandy, a bottle a day. No bloody good, boy. Life was a bloated blur. A buffalo's breath in winter, as the man said.* In a blink it would be over. His brain was Brie. Before he finally kicked the bucket he became a Buddhist. On his besmeared, brittle deathbed his eyes began to bulge and blaze like Beelzebub, and in beatific tones, brandishing a bayonet, the bum brayed: "Behold, my birlinn cometh to bear me o'er the cosmic brine". Wouldn't bank on it, Bladhmann.

*Attributed to the First Nation orator, Crowfoot.

GABRIEL ROSENSTOCK, member of Aosdána, is a poet, haikuist and translator. His latest book, from Cló Iar-Chonnachta, is the selected poems, *Rogha Dánta*.

Cathal Ó Searcaigh

"That night, the bristling clouds ..."

That night, the bristling clouds –
   those humped grey beasts of the sky
bared their sharpened claws and howled
   in a fearsome pack across the earth.
Their long fangs of rain, their barbed
   teeth of ice gripped the city, tore into
the tender flesh of life. In the dim light
   the night was a nasty, snarling thug
brandishing a broken bottle in a narrow
   alleyway. The moon, the bright companion
of my labouring nights was a ghastly
      skull peering in at me ominously.
That night, the dark at the heart of things
      came forth in fury.

And you, my Beloved, came from the night.
      You entered my darkened room, the secret
room at the core of my being. You lit it
      with the lamps of your gleaming eyes.
You sat me at the glowing hearth
      of your affection; you touched me
with the sweet song of your kindness.
      you caressed my human heart
with your gentle smile. That night
      you bathed my weary limbs in the
warm divine waters of your love
      my young god of life, of lust,
you filled my cup of solitude
      with the red wine of passion.
That night, my angel of light, you stirred
      me with life and death.

"Nuair a chan tú m'ainm ..."

Nuair a chan tú m'ainm, a chroí,
i mbogosnaí an cheana, ní m'ainmse a bhí
ann níos mó ach bláth an tsíolastraigh
          ag buíú i mbéal na gaoithe.

Nuair a theann tú mé le do chroí
i mbarróg fhiáin an ghrá, chan mise a bhí
ann níos mó ach sruthán samhraidh
ag brúchtadh is ag briseadh bruaigh.

"Éiríonn na focla ..."

Éiríonn na focla as mo chroí
ina n-éanacha uaigneacha trá
agus lorgaíonn dídean na hoíche
i nduilliúr craobhach do ghrá.

CATHAL Ó SEARCAIGH, internationally celebrated Irish-language poet, playwright and travel writer, has published numerous works including *Homecoming/An Bealach 'na Bhaile* (Cló Iar-Chonnachta, 1993), *Na Buachaillí Bána* (Cló Iar-Chonnachta, 1996) and *Ag Tnúth leis an tSolas* (Cló Iar-Chonnachta, 2000). Arlen House brought out a volume of critical essays on Ó Searcaigh's work, *On the Side of Light* (2002) and in 2005 published his early poems, *Na hAingle Ó Xanadu*.

John Montague

Encomium

Sometimes, unfortunately, one spends part of one's old age writing epitaphs, but it is far more pleasant to be composing encomia for one's friends of long date. For a while I contemplated sending a McDaid's blast of the kind our old master, Kavanagh, specialised in. But the truth is that I have always found James Liddy to be generous to a fault and gifted with an unusual sense of fun, even Blakean excess.

He also intersected with two of my old American friends, Melvin Freidman, a fine Beckett scholar I knew from gloomy Yale, and lonely ambivalent poet I knew from Iowa and San Francisco, William Dickey. Liddy seems to have an unjudging gift for friendship, and I was touched by his care for these two very different men, writing to me, for instance, after their deaths.

Long ago, *Arena* seemed to me to have lived up to its name, gaily gladiatorial. James worked out, for example, that the Master of Mucker could be inspired by a cheque, as well as a long-haired woman. And he featured my own "Siege of Mullingar" as a kind of Stop Press vision of a new Ireland, a month after the event.

On reading tours in the States I would always try to pass by Milwaukee because the Liddy experience always cheered me up. With my stammer I find readings difficult, but James always made sure that I had the right amount of petrol in my psychic engine. And the parties afterwards were un-American in their gaiety.

John Montague was born in Brooklyn, New York, in 1929 and reared on the family farm in Co. Tyrone. His poetry includes *The Rough Field* (Dolmen, 1972), *The Dead Kingdom* (Dolmen, 1984), *Time in Armagh* (Gallery Press, 1993), and *Collected Poems* (Gallery Press/Wake Forest University Press, 1995), among many others. A member of Aosdána, he lives in Co. Cork.

James Liddy

"Cypressed ..."

Cypressed
Yet moonlight on the cemetery
   is a comfort
Durable wood
Dense dark foliage
Baudelaire's Creoles "...fragility,
   the slenderness of their bodies,
      their velvety eyes ..."
Signs of mourning
The moonbeams sheening
The gates of Constantinople stood a
   thousand years
Turning death into jewellery
In New Orleans they used cypress shingle
I wanted to give my body at each corner
   I left it to death (the
   old country)
   What I kissed
      Were my pieces of gold
      The mouths more sinner than sailor
      I entering ...
      Where has love gone? To what cemetery?

from *Corca Bascinn* (1977)

MICHAEL S. BEGNAL

"Love's sperm & death's sperm": *A View of* Corca Bascinn *and* Comyn's Lay

Love and death: a poet reaches the end of his thirties and a sense of mortality creeps in. Suddenly the ominous inevitabilities can no longer be put aside the way they can be in one's twenties. West Clare is where James Liddy walked in the shadow of death, and his collection *Corca Bascinn* (1977) records the crisis (as George Stanley has called it: "a crisis of what meaning love can have when the world, at midlife, inverts itself"[1]), and its resolution through sensuality and through the poetic act itself.

Corca Bhaiscinn is the Gaelic name for the region of West Clare south of the Burren, a region marked by rocky shores and sea cliffs, described on the flap of the original Dolmen Press edition of *Corca Bascinn* as being "gothic" in appearance. In the first section of the book, SHORE, the wondrous landscape provides a setting upon which human experience may be elaborated. The shore is both real and unreal – it is a liminal space, the edge between land and sea, and gateway to the "Otherworld".[2] It is also a place charged with sexuality, where "[t]he tips of the fronds become swollen/The tide comes in they fuse to make spores" (12), where anemones swim in rockpools and beautiful youths walk the beach. The desolation of death and the frenzied activity of sex, at once!

Anemones, for Liddy here, are the quintessence of beauty ("the most beautiful animals of the sea shore/mistaken for/Flowers"[12]), but also stand as a metaphor for a poetic method:

> As in poetry
> As in the beginning [...]
> As in rockpools or on the seabed
> Complex structure is a disadvantage.
> Sea anemones with nothing corresponding to a brain... (11)

Here, loosely connected series of poems form sections, poems which resonate with each other, perhaps, or follow on from where another has left off. These loosely connected sections cohere to form the book. This is a long "serial poem", as originated and defined by Jack Spicer (one of Liddy's great heroes). "A serial poem, in the first place, has the book as its unit", said Spicer. "And you have to go into a serial poem not knowing what the hell you're doing ... It has to be some path that you've never seen on a map before. I think all of my books as far as they're successful have just followed the bloody path to see where it goes ..."[3] Meaning accrues in layers, almost of its own accord.

The second section of *Corca Bascinn*, SHRINE, sees the explicit emergence of religious themes, specifically the tension between (and the mingling of) paganism and Irish Catholicism. Liddy's going to get eschatological:

> What is this a rehearsal for?
> Is there a centre or set point of our endlessly
> revolving Celtic being or have we been
> poisoned with no magic for a thousand
> years? Look.
> We have seen the fish.
> Let us breathe about one of the changes after
> Death. (16)

At the start of the poem just quoted, Liddy harks back to the Finn cycle of Gaelic myth: "Finn cooked a salmon/Burnt a thumb and magic came/like one of his hounds". As Dáithí Ó hÓgáin has pointed out, the hero Finn MacCool is originally not only divine but is a poet as well: "Wisdom, in ancient Irish culture, was expressed in the form of poetry and magical knowledge and ... these gifts were primary aspects of Fionn's image. It is significant that the epithet *fionn*, meaning brightness, was often attached, in early Irish literature, to the craft of poetry".[4] Furthermore, Ó hÓgáin continues, "we assume that in archaic Irish lore Fionn had the function of visiting the realm of the dead in order to gain knowledge. This is a shamanic practice which is well-documented among primitive peoples, and Irish tradition itself furnishes much evidence of it. This includes the rituals engaged in by poets, such as composing in the dark and near mounds and raths, as well as the wide antiquarian knowledge the true poet was expected to possess".[5] Like the hero/poet Finn, Liddy returns to the basic roots of poetry in visiting this realm of dead ancestors (note that Liddy's mother's forebears were from Clare). Like Spicer, who held that his serial poems were in some sense "dictated" from without, Liddy in *Corca Bascinn* wants to listen to the voices of the dead. Liddy himself has written on Spicer: "It is simply a message, stark and reductively absolute as, the life lived, the craft eclipsed, last statements or testaments are wont – a message if it comes from anywhere, of ghost voices from under the world".[6] Spicer himself, in a chance instance of symmetry, was aware that W.B. Yeats (another of Liddy's great heroes) "is probably the first modern who took the idea of dictation seriously".[7]

Finn's fish (the salmon of knowledge) has later resonances. "Did you see the Jesus fish?" asks Liddy. The natural rock-pools of the shoreline transform into something else altogether: "If a god does breathe in the pool?/I try to get dead drunk on the/Thousand hints of an absolute divinity"(17). For Liddy, the paganism of Gaelic Ireland is not at odds with his own amoral interpretation of Christ and Catholicism – "Like the fun we have in the bar is our/Mass/Imitating/Explaining/Withoutness" (18). Or:

> The green drunkenness of Jesus
> In the water under the lush field
> We are drunk
> From the waves the perverted
> Angels sing on with open wings. (19)

With the explicit reference to John 5:2 of the New Testament, the pool can also be the pool of Bethesda where Jesus heals "a certain man", a pool of healing in which the poet, plagued with thoughts of mortality, seeks to immerse himself (20).

For all of Liddy's well-advertised Catholicism, however, *Corca Bascinn* is not really so much a Christian poem. It is, it seems to me, somewhat more at home in the milieu of Ireland's aforementioned native pagan religion. In section three, OCEAN, the poet imagines the "[d]ead swim[ming] back from the islands", wishes to "[s]ee what has come to us from the otherworld ..." (21). Like that most ancient Irish poet Amergin, Liddy imagines himself merging with the forces of nature – here the sea – and asks himself the question, "In what manner do you pray?" He then immediately answers: "Undress/Cross the wavelets. As foam" (23). In contrast to the social conservatism of contemporary Catholicism (symbolized by the "[b]ells of churches in Corca Bascinn"), Liddy entreats the fairies: "Dance again fairies of old/Who freed us from marriage rings of gold" (24). The word "fairies" is of course a *double-entendre*, the implication being that homosexuality too (not only a poetic paganism) is a means of freeing oneself from the strictures of Catholic sexual morality. As Brian Arkins has noted, Liddy explicitly affirms "the validity of sexual desire", a desire which "is Gaelic and pre-Christian, and was to be vigorously suppressed by the Catholic Free State that came into existence in 1922".[8]

In SANDHILLS, the figure of Donn makes his appearance. Though introduced as "[o]ne of the fairies of Doughmore", Donn is also in fact a major Gaelic underworld god, "[h]is powers from beyond the sunset" (27). Cousin to this death god is Angus, the god of love, who travels the glenside

Of a longing so intense
You breathe obstruction between lovers' parts
Thrilling the thick tongues of
Patrick's following
Who make love abstract
Not a passing hard on. (31)

So once again the interplay of these two themes (love/death, in the personages of Angus and Donn) is revealed as the underlying pattern of life, or shall we say that it is by embracing both sides of the coin that the world-weary poet will discover the key to his symbolic rebirth. Donn is throwing a party, or rather a sort of orgy: "Your ringed fingers rise the wand for the party/Swarm of bodies through rushlight/Harpers and young men" (31). The speaker is there too, partaking; like Orpheus he has descended to the underworld, or in this case the Celtic Otherworld, and has listened to the music of the fairies. As a result, and in keeping with a common motif of Gaelic tradition, he is imbued with the gift of poetry as well as a deeper knowledge of death (these are intertwined[9]) – the poet is initiated to the mysteries; he is somehow marked out.

After the carnality of the party, what? The bleak images of BIRDS, the cormorant on the rock – "beautiful killer through the sin of Adam" (33) – the passing of sensuality into the abstraction, the ideal of death – "Wild curlew whistle I offer my death to/Take me out of these false shadows" (36) – memories of dead friends and lovers, and the realization:

Now more thrilling
For his death which turns my love
As it should be turned
To death

This is my love story
My dead friends
All my friends will die... (36)

And in the CLIFFS section, the lesson of history – that change is the only constant, that nothing remains, not the heroes of the previous age, not civilizations, but perhaps the "Danaan gods" (as they have remained in

Ireland despite the arrival of Christianity), or the rocks and cliffs themselves: "I'm happy on the cliffs/'Above the real'/Because they last with slight modif/ications the way they/are" (43). And perhaps art?

The LOVE SONGS OF CORCA BASCINN, a five-page sequence beginning with the temerarious lines,

> Like any wandering pervert
> Any discussable struggling bard
> I walked the threads of the web
> In vague choirs of mickery
> Through veils of inspiration/dictation
> Promiscuous for action -
> The apparition/apparitions came
> And made me their plundered child (45),

summarizes many of the themes explored heretofore. Likewise, HISTORY further extends those of CLIFFS – with the translation of an excerpt of Clare Gaelic poet Michael Comyn's avid Fenian lay, with "Proverbs of Corca Bascinn" (which imagines William Blake as an Irish bard, and satirizes contemporary Ireland, Swift-like), with the poem "I.M. GEORGE FITZPATRICK", and with the brief lament for the vanished Anglo-Irish, "The Anglos have gone..." It is as if Liddy wants to examine himself in the scheme of local history once more before he departs for a new world. The final part of the collection is in fact EXILE, a sort of coda and almost a farewell to Ireland, which now becomes internalized as the locale switches to New Orleans: "Trees smell from bar homewards/hookers at Dauphine & St. Ann [...]/Gimme a drizzly Kilkee day with a breeze/And a pint of Smithwicks in it ..." (60). The romanticizing action of memory, perhaps, but Liddy is more matter-of-fact than misty-eyed Irish-American: "I left it to death (the/old country)" (63). And, at any rate, at least "In Exile a gay bar they put/Fresh orange juice in our screwdrivers" ("FOR BOBBY HAND") (62).

Although Liddy has always returned to Ireland, and so can't truly be said to be in permanent "exile", for anyone who has left for a substantial period the "old country" can become a concept, or an abstract idea, to be re-examined from another angle in time and space. As Liddy has said in an interview,

> As regards to what America does, I think it provides the escape from Ireland. It's the emigration thing. You're bringing your country with you, inside you, inside your mind – bring it over there! – and reassembling it, you know. I think that the distance is the distance of the Atlantic Ocean, and it's also the

> distance you have from your past as you grow older. You have a strong past, but you also have a different perspective on it. There's immense distance there. But the American part – what is America? America is to the Irish writer, or should be, a form of liberation.[10]

So with the final section of *Corca Bascinn*, Liddy announces a critical development in his poetic career. The idea of exile, of elsewhere, is now as important as Ireland. Ireland has symbolically taken on an identification with death, while New Orleans, with its social freedom, that of the promise of new experience. In response to the crisis postulated in the earlier sections of the book, Liddy makes a lateral, liberating move – he will no longer wait dolorously in the shadows of ancestors and tradition, but instead create a new world expanding out from older confines: "Is there a way of/Having a real country/Or do you just travel frontiers, man?" (64). In terms of technique, the liberation that Liddy finds in American society is paralleled by the growing influence of Spicer and other American poets, and thus *Corca Bascinn* stands as a turning point in his oeuvre. With the collection's final line, "Love's sperm & death's sperm", he compresses his main themes into four words and an ampersand: renewed creativity, the fruit of both love and death.

Many of the same poems in the last three sections of *Corca Bascinn* (i.e. LOVE SONGS, HISTORY, and EXILE) go on to form the bulk of Liddy's next publication, the chapbook *Comyn's Lay* (1978). In the context of the earlier, longer collection, these poems seem to reiterate the general themes previously explored (as noted above: LOVE SONGS returning to love/death material, HISTORY a re-situating of the speaker in the scheme of Irish history, and the title EXILE is self-explanatory). But since these pieces, or most of them, form the basis of *Comyn's Lay*, it's clear that Liddy also sees them as somehow different from the rest of *Corca Bascinn*. Otherwise, why the need for the later chapbook? He wants to revisit the process leading up to exile and the initial experience of exile itself, to get at it from another angle, feeling perhaps that he had not quite given it its full due. The cover photograph (by Herbert Kubly) shows Liddy with Jim Chapson at the grave of Joyce, that most famous of Irish literary expatriates.

There are only three new works here – a short prose piece (the "beginning of a novel found in the thatch of a cottage at Cooraclare") and the two poems "For Joe Marrone" and "For the Playhouse". The poem which serves as the conclusion to *Corca Bascinn* ("There's no keeping faith with ...") is now given the new title "Far from the Banner

County" and appears third to last here. The new poem "For Joe Marrone" contains the lines, "DeEmeraldised I love/Prostitutes and black queens",[11] which reinforces the otherness of Liddy's early American vision and his alienation from Ireland.

Given the chapbook's title, however, a certain emphasis is thrown back onto the Fenian tale of Oisín and Niamh, as translated from Michael Comyn's Gaelic lay. There is no contradiction in this. Oisín is in exile from Ireland when he ventures off to Tír na nÓg (the Land of Youth) with the goddess Niamh (the "streaming lady" of the poem). Tír na nÓg was conceived of as someplace other than Ireland, a place you could leave Ireland for, albeit only through supernatural means: "Let us steal softly out of town,/Oisín, until we reach my place" (*CL* 15). But poetry was *also* originally conceived of in supernatural terms,[12] and suddenly the tale of Oisín doesn't seem very far from Liddy's other major theme in these books, personal rejuvenation through art. Thus Oisín can be identified with the speaker of the other poems (the personage of the poet Liddy), who also leaves Ireland in response to the "crisis" of middle-age. It is significant that the relatively short excerpt of Comyn presented here deals only with Niamh's desire for Oisín and their initial flight, not with Oisín's return to Ireland and mortality:

> You have my spell on you, Oisín,
> You are a hero and now my husband
> Get up on my nag and we'll ride
> To the cosmetic suburbs of rejuvenation. (*CL* 15)

Although we know what happens later in the story, what we get here is the thrill of departure, in keeping with much of the rest of the chapbook.

With the conscious reordering of the *Corca Bascinn* poems in *Comyn's Lay*, Liddy moves away somewhat from the unconsciously dictated process of Spicer which he assumed in the former volume. But this seems necessary if he is to avoid being simply redundant. Where *Corca Bascinn* is a powerful work of inspiration, the very existence of *Comyn's Lay* (derived as it is from the preceding volume) means that it has to be seen as a comment upon the earlier work to some degree. Each can stand on its own, and each can be seen in relationship to the other, but they must be read differently from each other despite their common themes: *Corca Bascinn* as an inspired, organic whole, seemingly giving birth to itself; *Comyn's Lay* as individual pieces grouped together, arranged by a controlling authorial presence beyond the speaker of the poems. And with the concluding poem of *Comyn's Lay*, "For the Playhouse", Liddy finally does return to the terrestrial "mongrel world (an alternative/destiny to the suburbs ...)" (*CL* 29) – that is, as opposed to the "cosmetic suburbs of rejuvenation" (which, as we know, Oisín will eventually find to be an unsustainable, and even undesirable, existence).

The initially troubling final line, "I become a Catholic church full of confessions and high" (*CL* 29) – troubling because it seemingly runs counter to the "pagan" viewpoint of the rest of the material – begins to make sense in this context. It does not mean that Liddy suddenly makes an about-face and accepts the morality of Church teaching as a resolution to his "crisis". The Catholic Church simply represents order, the order that Liddy as an artist ultimately brings to his work and to his life, the order necessary to mediate the visionary poetic experience, which, however liberating, can also raise the danger of leading the poet into a permanent Tír na nÓg: fantasy, excessive abstraction, detachment from the real world of death and ageing, and avoidance of the conflicts which lead to personal growth and evolution. *Comyn's Lay* is, then, a coda to *Corca Bascinn*, but also a formal resolution of its own.

NOTES

[1] George Stanley, "Beyond the Sublime: Reading James Liddy", *Irish University Review* 28 (1998): 100.

[2] James Liddy, *Corca Bascinn* (Dublin: The Dolmen Press, 1977), 9. Future references to this work will be noted in parentheses in the text.

[3] Jack Spicer, "Excerpts from the Vancouver Lectures", in Donald Allen & Warren Tallman, eds., *The Poetics of the New American Poetry* (New York: Grove Press, 1973), 233.

[4] Dáithí Ó hÓgáin, *Fionn Mac Cumhaill: Images of a Gaelic Hero* (Dublin: Gill & Macmillan, 1988), 4.

[5] *ibid.*, 17.

[6] Liddy, "A Problem with Sparrows: Spicer's Last Stance", *Boundary 2*, Vol. VI, No. 1 (Fall 1977): 260.

[7] Spicer, "Excerpts from the Vancouver Lectures", *The Poetics of the New American Poetry*, 227.

[8] Brian Arkins, *James Liddy: A Critical Study* (Galway: Arlen House, 2001), 26.

[9] See, e.g., Dáithí Ó hÓgáin, *An File: Staidéar ar Osnádúrthacht na Filíochta sa Traidisiún Gaelach* (Baile Átha Cliath: Oifig an tSoláthair, 1982).

[10] Michael Begnal, "Interview with James Liddy", *The Burning Bush* 8 (Autumn 2002): 22.

[11] James Liddy, *Comyn's Lay* (Berkeley: hit & run press, 1978), 28. Further references to this work will be noted in parentheses in the text.

[12] Again, see Ó hÓgáin.

MICHAEL S. BEGNAL

Homage to James Liddy

It might be that Ireland is an illusion,
   Brazil,
disappearing into western sea haze
         beyond Aran

it might be that America is abstract,
   doesn't exist,
falling in the mind a decadent city
         beyond Aran

yet somewhere someone foots a lane,
a tangible cobble/someone
stands on the corner of the boulevard,

and we give them our respect,
for we are not so fortunate
         to be poets

MICHAEL S. BEGNAL (b. 1966) is a poet and editor of the Galway-based literary magazine, *The Burning Bush* (1999-2004). His first collection, *The Lakes of Coma*, appeared in 2003 from Six Gallery Press. His second, *Ancestor Worship*, will be published shortly by Salmon Poetry. He is also included in anthologies such as *Breaking the Skin: New Irish Poetry* (Black Mountain Press) and, in Irish, *Go Nuige Seo* (Coiscéim).

JAMES LIDDY

On Loop Head

Nothing above board
nothing lost not even loss for ever
nothing – pardon – academic.
Messengers disguised as drinking pals is
   everything
cosmic or comic ray like a piano and accordion
   in a fey house is everything
Cú Chulainn's leap is everything and a great day
   at the mouth of the Shannon.
Something that doesn't get us ready for River
      Tryst
something that made it easy to get laid in the
   house in Kilkee (if you've kept the photos
   from the beach)
something in the lost dialect that would have
      written this better.
Anything is seeing one in a crowd
anything like this morning a green parrot in
   cage with a MacCurtin hangover bardic head-splash
anything is your friend's wallet of dreams
   that you lost.
A certain thing
lover light and power more than a monk's hut
   on the island
lover passion has more waves than beloved passion
I have bathed you in it like a swan not on his
   final song on the estuary

I am Clare's son with drink taken that's why
   I am a sure thing.

previously unpublished

JIM CHAPSON

The Villagers Are Angry

Two old poets have set up house
on the hill above our Pure Land shrine.
They welcome their crazy wandering friends
with every outrageous civility.

How dare those drunkards carry on
giving a bad name to our village.
We work to support our families with dignity
while they go carefree, laughing like spirits.

Madeira Memento

Let me take a photograph
of you beside the pool.

I will keep a copy, call it
"you beside the pool",

and give you one which you will call
"me beside the pool".

Snowflakes

Spiky hexagons descend
from the world of ideal forms

glitter on my coat

At a touch
they shatter and melt

Fr. Hopkins

Misplaced
in the ironic
Irish earth

JIM CHAPSON was born in Honolulu in 1944, of English, German, and Portuguese ancestry. He has been for many years an Oblate of the nearly defunct Order of the Flaming Heart.

ZACK PIEPER

Good Friday (for James Liddy)

Look, the truth is I kept believing I was Rimbaud. No doubt just another one under the bedsheets with a flashlight. Talking dirty to an empty picture frame. I caught jealous bullets with my teeth instead of my wrists. Chicago & Detroit my African droughts. Of course the trouble with doing the aftermass crawl around all these ex-railroad towns is that there's a big iron nail instead of a pin on all the church doors & boutique shop windows. Their insipid petitions & bake sale penance. Hence: our mutual hangover.

This history in the trough of it, laments on car hoods, little banners to wave away. The Armenian baker's daughter singing to herself in the shower. Pointless vigils, countless desert retreats nix the singalongs. This little light of mine: I spit at it & waited for a silence to stir.

Tomorrow night the incense down the aisles. The God Head billows. Slouched in the back pew during Bishop Weakland's homily. You beseech me to take note: where there's smoke there's fire. When the other altar boys & I used to perform flawlessly, we got to finish off whatever vintage was left over in the tabernacle & later on spill our guts all over the football field's sheets of snow for tomorrow night's tidy spotlights.

Landscaping
for James Liddy

What this backyard's sacred tree has made
Is none of our business.
Neither are the seeds it spills
Out here in the so-called called cinematic mists.

Just dim those floodlights like they say
   & we would be in safe hands
To stop all these installations, repairs,
   side effects, tunnel visions &
Just flash each other! For the
Hell of it! Y'know, get it
Over with.

ZACK PIEPER was born in 1981 in the German-American town of Mayfield, Wisconsin. He has published in magazines, read at Woodland Pattern, is a friend of Alice Nutley. He is also a waiter at Brady Street Pharmacy, Milwaukee, where at dinner gather friends of Jack Kerouac, and Bob Watt.

Eric Adams

In the Shop

The air is a composition of smoke and chatter. Through it cuts her high-pitched laugh. She roams back and forth, filling the needs and dreams of those that come to her behind the pet shop. Above her lies an inscription on the dull white walls: "Strangers are friends you have not yet met". She smiles flower lips and peers at each in curious observation. At the end of the bar sits the familiar. She brings him a pint.

"Ah yes. My death arrives from the hands of the angel herself", says the poet.

She gives him a sideways glance. "What about your hand? All poets need their hands!"

He carefully sets the swollen limb on the bar. "That's fine. You can be my queen of euthanasia". The poet smiles with tiny eyes. "You need not worry; I have the spirit of a twenty-two-year-old virgin".

She gives him her mother's eyes. In crumpled piles lies his money. Her small hands thumb through it. Smoothing out each bill and stacking them neatly in front of the poet she speaks of the deceased lawyer. The poet looks up with lines running through his eyes, toward his lips.

"Oh Paddy, might I buy some eternal sleep from the Angel behind the pet shop!"

Towering and clean, the grey bricks pile on one another up to God. Saint Louis never saw this one coming. Beneath the enormous façade of the western entrance: the archbishop tries on his outfits – gold, purple, black and purple buttons. The show blocks my entrance to the place. But three poets storm the doors, ahead of me, and we are in. Inside is bigger than outside. Walls and pillars, marbled and glittered all the way up to the mural – stricken arches. Pére Marquette presides over all within the vast cavernous house. One goes to confession, two go to the front, I go downstairs.

The stairs are carpeted – the walls plastered. The hallway beneath recalls Metavante, a bank-worker's office. Behind the door of reprieve – a high school bathroom, little off-white tiles, the latest in commercial waterworks and an occupant washing his hands. I hide in the stall. There, as if this one were chosen for me, a coin – a penny – at the bottom of the bowl.

ERIC ADAMS was born in 1978 near Madison, Wisconsin. Some of his ancestors hailed from the Orkney Islands. He is a teaching assistant in the English Department of the University of Wisconsin-Milwaukee.

KEITH GAUSTAD

To an Irishman in Milwaukee

I will not be ashamed of how I voted in 2000.
This isn't phallic Florida,
This is Wisconsin:
the balls of the nation.
Named such as it has been known to swing a bit.
Peace, I say to you
conversos have married the Masons
and for once it may be for the best.
I promise to give *Portrait*: Chapter 5 a try
– Still warming up to chicken livers
and drinking as much as you.
So long as the grains
be as pure as the granules
we'll look forward to more corner bars.

KEITH GAUSTAD is currently a student at the University of Wisconsin-Milwaukee. He collaborated with James Liddy on a chapbook called *Songs on the Plane Carrying Hess from Germany* (Teppichfresser Press, 2004).

ROBERT WATT

Taking Fear Out of the Air

My ancestors.
Years of farming Scotland,
Wales, Ireland, Wisconsin.
Exchanging and mixing
emotions with horses, cows,
and chickens in flying feathers
of horse logic.

Flying feathers of roadway
chickens and grandfather dreams.

Flying horse logic
of green island.

Animals take fear out
of the atmosphere, that
is their real function,
if we don't scare them too
much to begin with.

Horses, cows and rabbits
will get us over our fear of
commies, fear of freedom,
fear of each other.

ROBERT WATT, a Milwaukee poet, has published eight books and painted over 500 paintings. He is also a photographer and has worked with thousands of artist's models.

John Thomas Menesini

Of Ink and Pulp

of ink and pulp
calls hymns
and we have benign seizures

betwixt the lines, a yalp by key or pen/
blue airy godspells
as egoist as Catholicism
stroke the braille of dead millenniums
sous encre/un Dieux
it all translated to the fucked up way I speak in
tongues based on Saxonist hybrids
Anglican Wing'd Godfoot

but trumpets ne'er looked better than Beardsley's idea
anyhow

Liddy is a rogue Catholic
a bookmark of creationism
Yin to Yang of Tibet ideal
in Rock
and Smoke
Mala Rosary
Implements of
Lasting intent of Lambwool and Skull Cups
Feed the Masses
Of Yourself
Sinners and Saints

a friend pointed out the lotus position most resembles
a cock and balls

pointing upward, base rooted
arown gold spurting

Yesu Phallus
   it's no wonder the Pope dresses in white
and so much importance is wrap'd about the fishes

JOHN THOMAS MENESINI's poetry collection, *The Last Great Glass Meat Million*, was published by Six Gallery Press in 2003. He currently lives in the city of Pittsburgh.

JAMES LIDDY

Allen Ginsberg 1982

Everything, in the moonshine diner
or in the heat of the lakes
of the University of Wisconsin
or in the turbot dinner
of the Village diner
or in the resistance to everything
except implicit temptation
or in sighs to the Lord
who may not be sitting there
in far-off cloud
or in the forbidden Pagoda
behind Buddha's Rangoon leaves
or in Robert Duncan moving through
the UWM Union attention focused
on the boys sleeping in chair or couch
or in refusing to dilute
early Don Quixote windmill material
or in the understated sweetness
of older men in love
to include real sugar daddies
or in their disguised sweetness
or in the nuptial shadows
of random Mark Anthonys
or in the wrist smeared with kisses
so many times of Morrissey,
or in Benjamin Britten's gold waistcoat
in goldfinch recitative
or in honeysuckle of last surrealist
or in honeyjuice of last Dionysian
compares to the shepherds falling
in love in *The Eclogues*

previously uncollected

PEARSE HUTCHINSON

Three Poems from the Italian of
Sandro Penna (1906-1977)
from Poesie *(Garzanti, 1989/1997)*

1.

The more I felt bound to you
the more I adored Nature
as if from a prison.

(A young woman calmly reading a book,
then watching
the sea for a long time from a high
balcony.)

But when you went away both sky
and sea
were false at midday, so I knew
my prison was my freedom.

(p. 448)

2.

He seemed all for me. But the kiss I gave
his red lips may have been clumsy.
Sudden and light he moved away
as the wind moves in April.

(p. 90)

3.

You needn't give yourself airs.
The only one I ever saw
with a right to such disdain
was the look in the eye
of a baby at a banquet
bored.

(p. 211)

PEARSE HUTCHINSON was born in Glasgow in 1927 to Irish parents, and raised in Dublin. His *Collected Poems* appeared in 2002 from Gallery Press, and he is a noted translator of Italian, Catalan and Galico-Portuguese poetry. He is a co-editor and founder of the literary journal *Cyphers.*

With These Hands

To make a catch. Make a catch and score. Those were my dearest wishes that Easter Saturday. I was dying for it. All het up for it. I'd go as far as to say there wasn't a mother's son in the whole club better turned out than me – I was a picture, even if I say so myself. Lord of all I surveyed, I set myself up commandingly on a high stool. It'll show my independence, self-possession, liberality. An official declaration of my availability to any brave one in the crowd. Like an attractive item in a shop window during a sale. I could enhance the advertisement later with signs added as necessary ... if necessary. All I had on was a black t-shirt, the height of fashion, with a bright image of Sinéad O'Connor on it, ripped 501's so tight you'd think they were sprayed onto me, and white trainers. I was clean-shaven with plenty of Fahrenheit on me. My hair slicked back with gel and well-groomed from this afternoon's wash. I was on for it, ready for the kill, as the bright young things here would say.

I hadn't been in such good form for ages, and it got better every time I lifted my pint to my lips or looked at the view from my high stool. There were loads of men in tonight, wee men, big men, and hunks too, by God, dancing and discoing before me – teenagers, men in their twenties, thirties and some older. I looked them over one by one – up, down, across, back, front. My own body was buzzing from top to toe, the blood swirling round my veins like cream being churned to butter. I was horny, really horny, my conscience-less cock directing my gaze all over the place like a heedless compass suddenly gone mad and loving it. I wanted something for Easter. Something sweet. Sweeter than sweet. Sure I'd have to go on the pull and score before the end of the night. But I knew I would. I believed in myself, in sunshine after the rain. It was a long time since I'd had so much faith in myself. You'd've thought I was high king of this really hip kingdom bopping and bobbing all around me – that every father's son was dancing for me with my royal prerogative – just like it was all translated from some magic dream by one of those *dei ex-machina*.

I knocked back another drink. Looked around me again. Boy, this place was hot, really hot. Not warm now, but hot. There was a "ra-bounce" going on on the dance-floor. Music, if you could call it music. Dance, if you could call it dance. A real wreck-the-house. Hip-hop and holler. A "desperate din" as the nuns used to say at school yonks ago. Heads, arms and whole bodies shook this way and that and sometimes right round as if they were swirling, twirling, spinning, hanging, dangling from the ceiling, under piercing strobes and rotating, multicoloured lights – others wobbled like geese, and then there were mysterious dark spots about which you could only speculate. Boy, half the ones here were high and the other half getting there.

And all the time, it was boiling hot and getting hotter. Everyone pressed tight together. Packed in, body to body. Me – I was checking out the ones in front of me with my bedroom eyes – sometimes all I could see was parts of them: heads, shoulders, bellies, nicely pointed behinds ... feet ... whatever turned up in the flashing lights. I knew some of the boys here one way or another – to see, to touch, some I knew well, others all too well ... but thank God there was a fair few new ones here, too. It was them I was most interested in. My glad eyes were drawn to them like magnets. I liked the new, the fresh, the "I'm not sure what type he is yet". O, to suss out a new man. A new man with a new body, a new mind ... everything new, maybe. A stranger! To move in on a stranger ... touch for him ... enchant him, dominate him, someone who could put me under their spell, too ... A special friendship, maybe ... more, perhaps. More than a one-night stand. You never know.

He was there! That is, if I could be sure in that crowd. I'd found him out with my keen eye on autopilot. He was in the corner the whole time like he was hiding on me. A big strapping fella, stocky but not fat, with a bright shiny shirt and dark trousers, short blonde hair and, in my opinion, gorgeous, about thirty, or nearly. No spring chicken, maybe, but he wasn't too old for me to have fun with. That's for sure. There was something different – fascinating – about him. Something very distinctive but I couldn't say just what it was. The shirt, maybe ...

Yeah, I was sure I'd never seen him in the club before, whether he was there or not, without me knowing. I wanted him right away. There and then. He really turned me on.

Who was he dancing with? I'd have to find out. What if he had someone with him? It was hard to tell for sure. One minute he was looking one way, the next minute the other – spinning right round. Maybe he wasn't dancing with anyone in particular, he was on his own and not with any crowd at all. Still by himself ... God, let it be so.

I took another drink. Stared hard to keep him in sight, chin propped on my hand, one leg balanced on the other. Hard. I'd keep with this one. He was still worth going for. Swaying about the whole time. All heart and legs, dancing and jumping. Sometimes he looked around. You'd've thought our eyes'd meet in silent acknowledgement or greeting, sooner or later. I was close enough for him to see me, to notice me watching him, if he wanted. If only the lights would hit on me for a minute. That wouldn't be easy. Mostly, they were blazing into his eyes and not mine, although they could turn around any second if they were bumped into. But he was as good as lit up by them the whole time – or so it seemed to me, anyway ...

What's this? Did I see some fella getting interested and checking him out from behind? Dancing right next to him? Moving in on him? I fucking did! The bastard. He just went ahead and rubbed his whole body against him. Familiar as you like, rubbed his hand up and down his behind just like that. Yer man moved quickly to one side, glancing over his shoulder. He looked to see who it was. He looked again, dismissively, to make sure. He drew back two or three steps ... A nod's as good as a blankety-blank. I took this as a warning. I'd have to be careful. And get a move on, too, maybe. There was plenty of other hawk eyes on the look-out. If you didn't shake yourself and do something quick, cast your net ... you could leave it too late. The worst thing would be to find out he was free and single only to see him snapped up by somebody else. I took a bigger drink. Set down my glass and got up.

I made it over to the edge of the dance-floor. Shook myself like a goat getting out of the water, just like the rest of them. I swayed and swung about, slyly winding my way through bobbing bodies over to the corner. In two minutes flat, I was right in front of him and knew rightly I'd hardly make a move as bold and sure as this one tonight. He hadn't noticed me yet. How could he've? He would soon enough. There was no getting away. The worst that could happen was just a knock-back ... I danced in front of him – sometimes coming very close. He had to see me looking at him, watching him, checking him out. With his right hand, he wiped a layer of sweat off his head, running his fingers back through his short hair till his elbow near stuck into me. It looked to me like he knew

I was watching him. I kept it up: the two of us dancing away. Gradually, our body movements fell into the same swaying rhythm ... Now my eyes lit up, ready to meet his, warmly, just as soon as he'd look at me, look into my eyes full of love and welcome. One second. That was all I needed. I waited and waited ...

Yes, he would have a drink, he said. He needed a break from dancing anyway. He was sweating. Water. That was all. He was driving and you had to be careful in the city. I never liked paying a couple of pounds for a bloody bottle of water when you could get something better for the same price. Ah well, each to his own, if that's what he wanted. Sure, the drinks were only an excuse anyway.

What was his name then? It didn't matter! Maybe it didn't matter but still it would be nice to know. To know who I was talking to. It was only polite – trying to get to know each other like any two people ... Maybe you're a Micky or a Dicky or even a Willy. He didn't answer but he smiled alright ... Well, my name's John Paul, if you really want to know; named after you-know-who, of course. I was born the day he came to Ireland, the poor sod. So! You're here with a man named after a holy father of the Church, even if he's not so holy himself. Make it Johnny, then, he said, bemused. Tonight, you can call me Johnny.

He wouldn't have a smoke either. He didn't like fags, at least not that kind, he confessed with another smile. He probably doesn't gamble either, I thought to myself. He's just what any mother'd want: a son who doesn't drink, smoke, gamble, or womanise ...

I asked where he was from, remembering I hadn't seen him before. The midlands. He obviously didn't want to be more specific. OK! I wasn't going to hassle him. It wasn't important. Up to the city for the weekend then, to get away for a bit? Not exactly. Just for tonight as he'd some work on tomorrow: a friend of his was away at a wedding and asked him to fill in for him. Working on a Sunday, I said, teasing him. A bad sign. A sin, too. Flying in the face of the laws of God and the Church, too. Sure, hadn't the bishops been up in arms about it recently? And they have to have their way, y'know ... Our eyes met. Some of us just have to work Sundays, he said, bishops or no bishops, and that's that. The world doesn't stop on Sunday for everybody. I agreed. What would happen if the Guards, nurses, doctors, bus drivers, bar staff, radio and TV people, etc. didn't work holidays and Sundays? Yeah, he was right alright. And even if he wasn't, I'd still've agreed.

I got the feeling he was shy, really shy, and not just letting on. That he was the kind of person you had to draw out of himself – something he then appreciated. But he was nice, and he had charm and sense, I thought. Yes, he was growing on me. It looked like we'd get on OK together. Because he didn't frequent this club, he didn't know anyone, he said. I gathered that he liked my company, my personality, the way I had about me and, yes, I may as well say it, my body, too – particularly my body. I thought I caught him glancing at my crotch a few times. Did he know I could see him ...? I caught his wandering glance for sure the second time. And he knew. Oh, he knew. And I was glad even though he looked away into the crowd. Shy again, maybe ...

Another round. More small talk. It was getting late, and I was getting worried. Time to speak up – put the cards on the table and ask. I was fairly good at this game. Confident. I believed in myself. I rarely asked anyone, if I wasn't sure of the answer. Tonight, I was extra-confident.

Soon the club would be closing – it was nearly two already. Would he go across the road for a coffee? Sure, he would – emphasis on the word "sure", I noticed. Brilliant! We exchanged a smile. Hot. I was getting horny again. I was there. I'd mastered the language. This rhythmical language of the body. Yes, I was proud of my handling of the language, my government of the tongue, my fluency in the bold outspoken language of the flesh that opened the way for communication and contact ... Anybody on for a coffee ...

Did I have a car? No. Oh, no problem. He'd see me home as well. A ride home would be nice, I thought. Where did I live? Southside. Oh, Southside. Even better. He was going that way himself – to his B&B. And where was I staying? My aunt's. Auntie Nora. My great-aunt, really, but we called her auntie. Pity I couldn't afford a flat of my own or a rented room even. Ah well. A real pity. Fuck all I could do about it now. Still, things could be worse. We had the car anyway. And left to our own devices ...

Then we kissed. Our tongues took over and reached for each other, pressed hard and longingly together. The two of us standing right at the bar. Locked together, in people's way and not even knowing it ... The two of us squeezed into one, almost.

We drove off. The grey city half-asleep that time of the morning and my right hand pawing away – at his knee, his thigh, his cheeks, his tackle – and him near ready to leap out of his skin like a jack-in-the-box as I fondled and fumbled away under the sleepy eyes of the city, pulling back my hand at red lights if anyone looked in on us, nosily. He was bursting for it: but what with driving, gears, indicators, and traffic lights, his left hand was busy most of the time – or, at least, it should've been ...

Did he know the way? The area? Yes, sort of. We were nearly there anyway. He'd been around here a few times before. He'd find it, alright. Some quiet side-street? *Cul-de-sac*? Beach? No. He knew a car park that'd be empty. He'd been in it once. Next on the right, he thought ... That was it. Another right again at the fork in the road ...

A huge square car park spread out before us. Is it for a supermarket? Not at all, it's a quiet chapel car park on a back road. They'd've thought we were robbers parked near a supermarket but a chapel wasn't worth robbing. He smiled. Where there's a chapel, there's bound to be a priests' house nearby. Maybe the priests would wake up. They'd drop dead if they saw ... It wouldn't be fair on a holy priest, especially an old one. He laughed. It wouldn't do any harm to open their eyes a bit – teach them about the outside world. But maybe we didn't even have to. Maybe they'd be into a secret night-time service. They're probably more used to this caper than we are ... if half the stories you hear are true ... I'm telling you. Some of them dropping off in private "bathing houses" around the city. Taking dizzy turns. Strokes. Heart attacks. Dying on the job even! All steamed up. On the night-shift, and what-have-you ...

He parked the car tight into a wall. This corner of the car park was dark and in shadow, the shadow of tall trees on the other side of the wall. There was a short silence after the engine wound down. A quick look round – just in case. There wasn't a sinner about. How could there be? We both had to get out of the car for a piss. Each of us at either side of the car – me on my side, him on his. As quick as we could. We got back into the warm comfortable car shutting the doors as quietly as possible, scared of wakening any creature alive or dead. For who'd be about that time of night or morning but a thief, drunk, or some other lovers ...

We held each other ... pawing ... petting softly. Radio 2, nice and low. We embraced awkwardly. I was squashed against the front dash, even though I could usually master and manoeuvre these small spaces. Could we move the seats back? Sure, and from the bottom, too. There was a knob down below. In the middle, between my two feet, or in the place where your feet would normally be! There was a tiny wheel at the side, just behind me, if I could reach ... my hand across ... Aah, that was much better, far more room.

What a great car, I said; you keep it nice. Some small talk was necessary. You must have a good job – an office job, I'd say. I squeezed his soft hands. They weren't exactly hands scarred and toughened by construction work, like my own. I let him rub them over my chest and belly, lapping up his gentle touch. I put my arm under his armpit to pull him over somehow to my side of the car till he lay on top of me nice and tight ... our two bodies one on the other, mouth to mouth, chest to chest, stomach to stomach ... We kissed hungrily. His full beautiful weight pressing down on me.

And you won't tell me what kind of job you have – apart from this one – I said, drawing breath and teasing him. I mentioned the fancy car again. God, you're a strange one. You must get a good wage. A lot more than I'll get for my handiwork tonight. I liked his way of talking. Or maybe you're married with a wife at home? Oh, sure. He'd five or six boys at the last count, he said. If he did, they certainly weren't allowed in this spick and span vehicle! Of course, I didn't believe a word out of him ...

We put our arms around each other and hugged real tight. We didn't move for a few minutes, simply savouring the moment together as lovers and strangers. It was good for both of us ... Then one of his hands started searching about – down between the two seats till he lifted something. I looked. A wee bottle. A bottle of holy water, is it, to throw over the car every now and then for protection? Well, well, well.

It's got to be done, I said, taking the poppers, now that the lid's open ... I took two deep sniffs of it – one nostril after another. I got an extra hot kick out of it right away. All at once, the blood went racing in my veins and my heart pounded like a hammer. He took some too, with a flourish. Oh, so the poor wee wife waiting for you at home must've got you that bottle, too; stuck it down into your pocket so you wouldn't forget on your way out. So she did, if she only knew. We'll need these as well ... soon. We'll soon have tears of joy, my boy! Mansize, I said. Good thinking ... Next thing we were wrapped in each other's arms again, more passionately than before ... it was now or never.

Right then, mate. How far was he looking to go – to fuck me, or for me to fuck him? Neither. He was firm about that. He'd no condoms anyway. Why didn't his wife stick a rake of them in his pocket? I'd a few on me somewhere, if I could find them. No need, he said. OK. I went along with him. In any case, it was right to be careful – especially these days. So, a hand-job. A hand and blow-job, maybe. "Come together". Right on. By this stage, he was down and I was on top without a stitch or a twitch of fear and the windows all steamed up for us by the strange mist of our breathing. His soft tender hands made their way between my legs to fondle my prick, gently, patting and petting over and under as he pleased. Then came lips and tongue – licking, all warm and tickly. I also took full pleasure in hand and mouth – fair play. We both had it in us.

Then, tensed in bliss, we both came in lunges, spraying wild jets of relief. Both coming together, fit by fit, almost.

It was as well he had the mansize tissues there, mopping up afterwards. They were our gift from the gods, and he was mine. We both laughed out loud from the very heart, and lay back.

Soon, it would be morning. We'd see the sun dance yet, perhaps ...

Number 77, I said, looking out the window. Over on the left – see that pink door? Well, it's not that one, but two down! I'm sorry it's not 69, but it's not my place, it's my aunt's. No sign of life – auntie Nora's slept half the night by now. I wouldn't be surprised if she drags me out of bed to help her to second Mass ...

Drive on. He went 200 yards down the road before he pulled in. He killed the engine.

My hand was on his knee. He put his on top, working his fingers in between mine, nice and tight. I turned my palm around so our fingers were bound together. We squeezed palms even tighter.

I felt so cosy then ... our hands touching each other, all tickly. I was more comfortable than I'd ever felt. It was like the blood had stopped in my veins. The passion before was nothing to this. Nothing. This peaceful calm was going right through me. I looked into his eyes, my moist palm tight against his. There was a stranger's kindness in that hold. Passing strangers on a wild dark night. I felt that, affection and loneliness all in one. Wasn't there more for me in life than this? The hunt and the one night stand? Like so many times before? Maybe it was time now to give up that transient but fun life. Time to ... Yes, I wanted more than just "action" ... I began to feel sort of grown up now ... Like I was a man now ... Maybe he was the kind of person I could settle down with, some day, if I got to know him right. He was different somehow from other men I'd met. I'd played the field and every position on it, I thought; my wild oats were well and truly sown. Young as I was, I still felt like sharing my life. I fancied a more permanent relationship. It was like I was wising up. It didn't bother me that he was nearly ten years older. Maybe he wanted something more serious, too – not to be always meeting like strangers but to see each other on a regular basis ... in the clear light of day.

But he didn't, which surprised me somewhat. Not that he didn't want to, but how sure he was about it. Maybe he just wanted a quickie 'cos he'd another man at home. He said no. Would I see him again? Maybe. If he was in town. No promises. He had his arm around my neck, his fingers playing with the back of my hair, while he kept an eye on the window and side-mirror at the same time. Didn't he have a phone number? Yes, and no. He couldn't give it. There were other people at the same number who had no idea. Too bad. Perhaps he really was married! But I'd be careful when I phoned. I could call at a certain time – whenever suited him. Day or night. Take a half-hour off work if I had to. It had to do with business. What business? OK, then, if he wasn't going to give it. I'd met plenty like him before. Did he want my number? He'd take it then, he said, writing it out with a biro off the dash. Between 8:00 and 9:00 was best, weeknights. If I wasn't in, say he'd call back. If he was asked, because of his stranger's voice, just say he got my name from somebody else 'cos he needed a wall put up out the back and needed a brickie ... but there was no hurry and he'd call back. Not to say what he'd seen already and that it was himself he wanted worked on. He laughed. Maybe he would call then. OK, he would ... sometime, when he was coming up to the city. It would probably be a month or two but he would call, if possible. He promised this reluctantly, only because I asked. I could see him in the club or wherever else he was. Some weekends I went home to the country. From now on, I'd be at the club every weekend. I wanted to keep in touch with him somehow or other. It meant a lot to me.

We sat in the car another few minutes, saying nothing. Neither of us wanted to break the silence. A kind of emptiness came over us, I think. Me, anyway.

We'd another quick hug before we parted. We kissed briefly again, once more – for luck – letting our tongues meet for just another split-second.

Then I got out. Slowly. Quietly. The cold struck me. There wasn't a soul to be seen in the streetlights. I took a deep, deep breath. Ruffled my clothes. Made sure my belt was done up. Straightened myself. I shut the door, telling him one more time I hoped to God I'd see him again before long ...

And so I did. The very next day from the back of the chapel – saying 12 o'clock Mass.

MICHEÁL Ó CONGHAILE was born in Inis Treabhair, Connemara in 1962, and is the founder and publisher of Cló Iar-Chonnachta. His short story collections include *An Fear a Phléasc* (1997) and *An Fear nach nDéanann Gáire* (2003). His novel, *Sna Fir* (1999), won the Bord na Gaeilge award at the Listowel Writers' Week Festival and Comórtas Sheáin Uí Éigeartaigh at the Oireachtas Literary Competitions. In 1997 he received the Butler Award from the Irish-American Cultural Institute, and the Hennessy Award. His play, *The Connemara Five* is published by Arlen House in Ireland and the US in April 2006.

Interview by TRENT HANSON

James Liddy, the Priest of Poets

LET'S TALK ABOUT WHEN YOU WERE IN YOUR THIRTIES IN IRELAND. AS A GAY MAN IN IRELAND, WHAT WAS THE CLIMATE LIKE AT THE TIME?

I don't think there was any climate except for the climate of alcohol. In a sense because of the climate of alcohol almost anything went because alcohol excites the passions and leads to creative situations sometimes. I think there was no particular bad climate because there was something more like alcoholic joy.

A GOOD FRIEND OF MINE ONCE SAID THAT SHE ROMANTICIZES THE DAYS BEFORE IT WAS ACCEPTABLE TO BE "OUT". THAT IT WAS MORE EXCITING BEING GAY BACK THEN.

Well I think that's right. Secrecy is a wonderful thing. Shadows and intrigue when it's not really out in the open is a vast business. And the subversiveness of it was apparent. Like in Milwaukee all the gay bars had back doors because people didn't want you to see them going in – particularly married men. So that seemed to me a lot more exciting. Besides, it seems to me that the current "out" thing, while good enough, is nothing but political. It doesn't fulfil aspirations of the heart.

WHAT ARE SOME IMPORTANT QUALITIES OF A GOOD POEM?

It's hard to say because what you think of at the beginning is not necessarily something that lasts. The quality of a poem is hard to define; it's almost impossible to define, save this – if something stays in your memory. If some part of that poem, some words of that poem, some sentence becomes part of your mental furniture and you think of it from time to time. Or if the language of the poem becomes kind of a verbal tune in your head, you know, you can always rely on it and give yourself some sort of insight or satisfaction. It's impossible to define what a good poem is because there's so many different kinds of good poems and there's so many, much more, different kinds of bad poems.

PAT JOURDAN

The Perfect Irish Poem

A field, a green field,
a field with a horse in it,
a white horse against the driving rain
with a wind-shorn tree in the sunset.
Some mountains;
settled in blue distance, a white cottage.
More fields scattered as far as the eye can see.
Weather (rain, hail, sun, mist)
and time (seasons, stars, moon, etc.)
provided free, self-maintaining.
The reader the only occupant
except perhaps some suitable peasants
going about their picturesque peasant-humble tasks,
off-centre, middle distance, blurred,
and of course, the patient horse,
the myriad, puzzling green vanishing points.

PAT JOURDAN is of Liverpool Irish extraction and studied painting at Liverpool College of Art, where John Lennon was her fellow student. A long-time Galway City resident, she recently returned to England. Her latest poetry collection, *Turpentine*, was published by Motet Press in 2004 and in 2005 her first short fiction collection, *Average Sunday Afternoon* was published. She is included in the anthologies *¡Divas! 2* (Arlen House) and *Anthology 1* (Ainnir Publishing).

Órfhlaith Foyle

Italian Nuns

In Kenya, we knew Italian nuns
Who snapped chicken necks
And swung pig sausage from the
Kitchen rafters.
They smelled of soup and incense
And dug their fingers into our cheeks -
A sign of endearment.
Dangerous women, we decided
And loved them back.
We dragged dead pigeons to their door
And walked barefoot in their rooms.
Sometimes they seemed to pray,
But when they called to the chickens,
My sister, brother and I
Sat, watched and waited.

Órfhlaith Foyle was born in Nigeria to Irish missionary parents; she now lives in Galway. Her début novel *Belios* was published in 2005 by Lilliput Press to widespread critical acclaim. Her collection of poetry and short fiction *Revenge*, was also published in 2005, by Arlen House.

JAMES LIDDY

Dear Anima, Show These Words

Without drowsy dust the wet, the brave.
Ocean sorrow greater than river melancholy.
Cloud plight, blood dawn test of the weak.
Talk, internal immigration, funeral bell.
Lack of repose like the lack of trees.
I feel like pollen; imagine feeling like pollen.

Triumphant forest of youth without trees.

Armada light of the past fades as
a mutual admiration society taps the road,
in heat, full of anticipations
about the possibilities of drink-life.
The awkward page. Detached – a resort
Lazarus – as if your echoes had already put
a wet mark on their lips. Ex-sphere.

But life after life county? The cost of living
is to reduce the cost of each kiss ...

The kiss. Remembering, panic-depressive
nativity, the form known as love (the
exterior brimmed back to the interior)? Descent
images of where they wind below the wall,
seaweed anemone hover points. Feet down
the legitimate concrete steps,
tragic with rocks' lines.

Dear Anima, summarise this resonance.

Have no respect, believe only
in immortal bliss of saved souls after just sexual
life. A more showery animal-ideal
than the just ordeals.

And, Mother, inside the house as I sit
on the seawall. You are a star, a cloud,
a hush hush wreath of moonlit water
and you must swim down there
away from the dark rocks to Purgatory.
I have the observance of the sexual life.

from *A White Thought in a White Shade* (1987)

MARY O'DONOGHUE

Clare Concerto
for James Liddy

The window, leaf-filled, is a picture
of hands flung up in a dance,
a frantic raking and combing of air.

There's a desperation of claws on wood:
the raccoon couple, staggery as drunks,
navigate back to their souterrain pad.

The night hiccups, then holds its breath.

But there is nothing so flagrant
as the frogs in Virginia, detonating
their desire in bawdy fat burps,

an orchestra of eructation.
They throw their voices over
the bridge. A she-frog audience is agog.

Going back further, other summers,
to cats on the hot slate roofs
of Kilkeedy. They shredded our sleep

with their hewling and mowling,
ululating worse than Huxley's
sexophones. We opened the window

to reprimand them, and filled

the room with their rallentandum,
the indignation of Jaffa, Felix, seated

on the capstone like a randy pillar saint.

MARY O'DONOGHUE was born in 1975 and grew up in Co. Clare. Her first poetry collection is *Tulle* (Salmon), and her work features in *The New Irish Poets* (Bloodaxe). She has received the Hennessy/*Sunday Tribune* New Irish Writing Award for fiction. She lives in Boston and is Assistant Professor of English at Babson College.

EMILY CULLEN

A Note on the Legacy of Patrick Kavanagh

Kavanagh relied upon, and trusted in, his parish as a worthy subject for his poetry: "The parochial is universal – it deals with the fundamentals", he wrote. By the time he composed his oft-quoted poem, "Epic" (1951), it was clear to him that Inniskeen was every bit as important as "the Munich bother;" a local feud involving old McCabe was as pivotal as the international politics of a super power! The privilege of being an adopted parishioner in Inniskeen has not been lost on me. Everyday I drive three miles from my apartment over undulating, narrow roads overtaking Shancoduff and Cassidy's Hanging Hill and I am privy to something of Kavanagh's dreamtime. It has come home to me that all the fundamental values on which great civilizations are based can indeed be found in the basic structure of the parish.

Like James Liddy, I feel indebted to Kavanagh for his celebration of the habitual in Irish experience. However, I will not permit myself to sentimentalise him. To me Kavanagh is a robust cultural complex of the human condition – both divine and fallacious, poor in the physical sense and abundantly rich in the metaphysical sense. He was a man of many parts, sometimes romantic in his attitudes to the natural world, often emphatically unromantic in his prose. He has both the "unprotected heart" of the poet and, yet, was not afraid to utter inflammatory indictments of contemporary writers, the Literary Revivalists, the post-Republic government, and so forth. A journalist recently asked me if I was "Kavanaghed out" after my eight months as Programme Director of the Centenary Celebrations in his honour. How could I possibly be? I responded, I have had a most rewarding year of discovery, continually refreshing my perspectives about the man. In many ways he was a sum of paradoxes: his love-hate relationship with the land, society and religion often extended inward so that he altered his opinions of his own writings over time, censuring both "The Great Hunger" and his first autobiographical novel, *The Green Fool*, later in life. His pronouncements on a variety of subjects, including that of his own "genius" were always unique and original but frequently contradictory. Any project that attempts to simplify this poet is flagrantly misguided.

On researching the legacy of Kavanagh what struck me immediately as something with which I could readily identify was his quest, both on a human and artistic level. His life's journey is a Plato's cave of the artist's development – moving from pastoral idealism, to realism and anti-pastoral, to satire and back to a lyrical celebration of the common things that are beloved. I believe that Kavanagh's journey is a helpful paradigm for younger writers because it is easy to delineate the path of his artistic development. The traditional motifs of the *bildungsroman* or quest novel were manifestly acted out in Kavanagh's aesthetic and personal journey: departure, initiation and return; leaving the countryside, seeking acceptance by the mainstream, disenchantment with convention and return to a lyrical celebration of what was native. Had he not passed through his anti-pastoral phase, the corpus of his work would be deprived of that great epic poem, "The Great Hunger", which articulates so truthfully the often harsh realities still attached to an isolated rural existence and the spiritual hunger so prevalent in contemporary Ireland.

I have absorbed much from the paradigm of Patrick Kavanagh in his centenary year. What he teaches me personally is to have the courage of my convictions. In this era of acute political correctness, when people are fearful of speaking definitively anymore, Kavanagh teaches us to speak our minds and "not to care" about pandering to others. This may not be a revolutionary idea, but to a well-bred, well-educated girl like myself it is nonetheless of significant import! Kavanagh was unequivocally honest and many say his honesty made him his own worst enemy. When I read his lyrical poems I am frequently struck by the fact that he was able to sublimate such infinite love and such a sensibility in the cantankerous exterior he so often bore around the streets of Dublin and the roads of Monaghan. Anthony Cronin, in his accomplished portrait of Kavanagh in *Dead as Doornails*, surmises that his ungainly gait might have been a kind of "social protest". He was installed in the capital as the authentic "peasant poet" and decided to burlesque this caricature as a kind of social commentary. I believe it may have been more of a protective shell for one who was extremely sensitive and often quite shy.

What I have probably learnt most from Kavanagh is that the pursuit of that vexatious abstract known as Truth must continue to be foremost in a poet's life. Needless to say I had gleaned this wisdom from Keats and Wordsworth long before, but somehow Kavanagh's idiosyncratic version of the truth seemed more accessible. Kavanagh held that "the purpose of the poet is to give people an enthusiasm for life" and "to excite the moment with hope". The fact that Kavanagh wrote about "the here and now" – not replicating the backward glance to heroic times like the Revivalists before him, but celebrating the present tense – continues to inspire me. In the same way that James Liddy is uniquely James Liddy, Patrick Kavanagh was Patrick Kavanagh alone – his own man, true to himself – ultimately inscrutable, but wonderfully original in every way. It is one of the tragedies of Irish literature that the gift of Patrick Kavanagh was not more widely appreciated during his lifetime. Without the recognition Kavanagh received from a core group of the upcoming generation of poets, including Liddy, Eavan Boland, Brendan Kennelly, Leland Bardwell, Paul Durcan, etc., there would be a palpable gap in the acknowledgement and passing on of the poet's work. Liddy has consistently acknowledged his own personal debt and Irish poetry's debt to Kavanagh. The momentum which this group created in tribute to Kavanagh was sustained as his poetry began to be promoted at Trinity College, UCD, and ultimately found its way onto the Leaving Cert syllabus.

Those disciples who bore witness in McDaid's pub must have helped to fuel his self-belief in difficult times of abject poverty and a hostile establishment. It is almost karmically apt that now the disciples of James Liddy are collectively celebrating his life and work in this unique book. Seamus Heaney has said that "Kavanagh's great achievement was to make our subculture – the rural outback – a cultural resource for us all. He provided us with images of ourselves".

We may be a predominantly urban and suburban society now, but Kavanagh's poetry still touches the quick of our culture and our national consciousness. I would reject any notion that his corpus is time- or site-specific to a rural Ireland of the 1950s. We know that the spirit of his work is eternal, reminding us that there is wonder in the commonality of our own everyday experience: "I turn away to where the Self reposes/In that placeless Heaven that's under all our noses" ("Auditors In"). Kavanagh relentlessly pursued the truth and the visionary and was prepared to fail now and then along the way. The nation holds its "poet of the people" in a wide embrace for many reasons, not least because he was an authentic individual, human, complex, euphoric in his liberation of Irish poetry and celebration of life, and because he struggled honestly with the vicissitudes of poverty, illness and finally, alcoholism. Kavanagh achieved universality on a whole new scale to redefine the parameters of

poetic reception, making poetry a non-exclusive art form which could be appreciated by the man in the street.

EMILY CULLEN recently served as Programme Director of the Patrick Kavanagh Centenary Celebrations. She was the inaugural Arts Officer of NUI, Galway, between 1999 and 2002, and has returned to the university as an IRCHSS Government of Ireland scholar at the Department of English, where she is studying for her PhD and teaching part-time. Her first collection, *No Vague Utopia*, was published by Ainnir in 2003.

The River Flows On

Going home. The hit of it. The bring-you-down feelings. Despite your happy childhood. Everything's the same but changed. You're like a giant in a familiar land; nowadays you find you must climb over the bushes instead of through them.

The gooseberry bush has been pulled from your favourite field. You circle the spot where it used to be, and miss the bitter bite of the downy globes, their tough sour skins. The apple tree you once fell from has been felled. You remember the thunk as you hit the ground and the dizziness you felt when you stood up. Two pines grow taller than you. Two pines that shouldn't exist because they don't share your history. The snowberry bush stands waiting for the snap and fizz of berries bursting between tiny fingers.

But the river flows on. Muddy and pungent and threatening. You call to mind the foul weedy stink you took home with you whenever you swam in it. The broken-bottle glass on the river-bed. The threat of whirlpools and dangerous currents. The drownings.

It's all a part of you. You own this part of the Liffey. This side of the bank, at least. The other side is a wilderness, as uncharted and deep as a tropical forest. The herons and the swans that wade and glide on this side of the river-bank are familiar to you. You know them. On the other bank lies a choking wilderness. Wolves slink through the trees, revealing only a silvery flank or the flash of a gilded eye. There are bodies caught in the rushes.

You pick wild garlic and chew on the stems, spitting the mulched clumps into the grass. You visit the ruins of the church, lifting the viney curtain from the entrance and bending to step inside. The smell of death mingled with damp earth sends you reeling. The corpse of a wild cat lies rotting among the stones, its mottled fur a heaving nest of maggots. So you turn and leave. You return to the river's edge to watch the swirling dance of leaves and twigs that are caught behind a fallen tree, their water journey come to a halt.

And you think of him. The workaholic aggressive that you chose from among all the men you knew. He who thinks you know nothing of his betrayals. His whitewashing. His reams of excuses. And you realize he doesn't know the first thing about you. Or the last. He doesn't know that the river is part of you, and that you are part of it.

So, you heave yourself into the water with a small laugh. Hoping for a cleansing. Or a whirlpool. You belong to the rushing water, its eddies and gushes. You delight in the undertow, the pull of the current when you glide past the spot where the mill race meets the flow. The riverweed wraps its velvety fingers around your ankles and slides up your thighs. The dankness engulfs your hair, and the metallic dirt of the water slips between your teeth, cramming itself into your waiting lungs. You feel yourself fill to the brim, and your head aches, but then there is a curious calm, so you smile.

You slip, quiet now, towards Chapelizod, past tree lined banks where fishermen are lost in their own reveries, and they don't notice you passing. Your arms float out from your sides like wings and you spin a little, your knees bent. Your shoes have found their rest on the sludge of the river-bed, and your wrists have picked up a trail of riverwrack bracelets.

If you were capable of thought now, you would be enjoying yourself. The slow pace of the water; the lift and fall of your co-operating limbs; the rushing hustle of the trees as you pass. Most of all you would be enjoying the view. The clouds scudding overhead in the unlit sky. Your own part of the river ebbing away and away while you float on through unknown territory. You would appreciate the patterns made by the half-light slipping through the canopy of leaves when you veer close to the river-bank. You would like the fact that the far bank is nearer to you now than your own, and that the wolves are sitting in easy groups, watching your progress.

You are languid now, cradled by the river that has rocked you to sleep. Your pace is slowing and the smile is falling from your lips. One foot snags on the branch of a fallen tree, and you spin for a moment before halting in the stagnant water gathered behind the trunk. The scurf that washes back and forth on the surface coats your hair. When your head is momentarily submerged by the ebb and flow, a twig settles itself between your open teeth. An eel glides through the crook of your arm, and hovers for a moment over the curve of your belly, before flickering on in search of food.

Restrained now, your movements become more sluggish. Your skin has taken on a pearly sheen and your arms lie limp. This is not the freedom you had hoped for; you didn't mean to be stayed so soon. Water skids and slides around and about and over you. You remain an unwieldy lump of flotsam, bobbing and ducking in the shadow of the fallen tree.

Until your absence is noted and with the quickening dusk worry sets in, and efforts are made to find you. To bring you back.

And the river flows on.

NUALA NÍ CHONCHÚIR lives in Loughrea, Co. Galway. She has won the inaugural Cúirt New Writing Prize (2004), the Cecil Day Lewis Award (2003), and the Francis MacManus Award (2002), and has twice been nominated for a Hennessy Award, all for fiction. Her first collection of short stories, *The Wind across the Grass*, was published by Arlen House in 2004 and is followed in March 2006 by *To the World of Men, Welcome*. Her poetry collection, *Molly's Daughter*, was published in the first *DIVAS!* anthology in 2003, and in 2005, Nuala edited the second volume, *DIVAS! A Sense of Place*, featuring 50 Galway women writers.

JAMES LIDDY

For Lorna Reynolds

The red climbing roses the fuchsia
of the Friends Meeting House Wexford,
friends whom you meditated on like Petrarch.
Bogcotton afloat in the swamp
before the Gulbenkian in Lisboa
by the gates a cluster of oleanders
whose bark sap makes people sick
like beauty worked at too much;
the stress the alteration predicted in the
breaking of the definite, that desperate radiance.

In Madeira among the different bougainvillea,
trees loaded with small bananas –
girls in flower in their Funchal dreams,
statues of gold and silver that speak to me –
I look over the pool with Vergil's Pastoral Poems.
If there is trouble in Paradise (there is)
a reason maybe women did not always confer
status on their surroundings; you had
bestowed the clear mind of a divinity,

this is simple: a garden, a gardener, flowers and bushes
I had seen the week you died, classical elegy.

previously unpublished

Brian Arkins

Dionysus Talk: Liddy's I Only Know That I Love Strength in My Friends and Greatness

In my book *James Liddy: A Critical Study* (2001), I dealt with Liddy's volumes of poetry up to and including *Gold Set Dancing* (2000). Since then Liddy has published a further volume of poetry, *I Only Know That I Love Strength in My Friends and Greatness* (2003), which I wish to consider in this essay.

Two stylistic features of this volume that have thematic implications are immediately striking: the use of asyndeton and the use of real people. The use of asyndeton – "a figure which omits the conjunction" (OED) – refers not so much to lack of connection within sentences as to lack of connection between different sentences or sections within a poem. The effect of such asyndeton is to require the reader to work out the connections between different elements for herself or himself, so that these poems of Liddy's provide a good example of how reader-oriented theory[1] can be invoked in understanding poetry. The poem "Dawn" will serve to illustrate the issue of asyndeton in Liddy:

> "Waugh was with me at Oxford
> he wore a yellow sweater everywhere
> he was a nancy boy ..."
>
> I look up to a bulldog face
> Christopher Hollis a Tory member
> of Parliament
>
> a Catholic – I've been a Catholic
> for forty years
> slouching in a yellow sweater
>
> morning and noon –
> yellow sweater not star for Jonathan
> yellow sweater not star for David
>
> Davy Byrne's pub a fragment
> forty years ago.[2]

The connections between the five sections of the poem work as follows. The writer Evelyn Waugh was at Oxford, was a Catholic, had Tory views, was called "a nancy boy", wore a yellow sweater. So too Christopher Hollis was at Oxford, is a Catholic, and is a Tory M.P. So too Liddy is a Catholic, is gay, and wears a yellow sweater that has no Jewish overtones. Liddy has been a Catholic for forty years and likes to drink, being found at the beginning of that time in Davy Byrne's pub in Dublin; Waugh also liked to drink. In the past, Waugh's Oxford, Liddy's Davy Byrne's, Catholicism, being gay, the yellow clothes constitute origins: hence the title of the poem "Dawn".

2

Liddy's poems in *I Only Know That I Love Strength in My Friends and Greatness* deal with many real people, particularly with writers and personal acquaintances; in this practice he is similar to Catullus (who appears in the poem "The Cabala") and to Yeats. Indeed the title of the volume comes from a poem by Jack Spicer called "A Poem without a Single Bird in It" (1956), while the poems themselves are designated on the title page "Wilde Centenary Poems" (a poem is also devoted to Wilde). Then a sequence of "Territorial Poems" deals with various antinomian writers: Enid Starkie and Rimbaud, Jarry, Burroughs, Kerouac, Spicer, Elizabeth Bowen and Medbh McGuckian, and Michael Hartnett. A longer prose poem is devoted to Yeats. At the same time, Liddy refers to other real people he knows: his mother Clare Reeves, the Archbishop of Milwaukee Rembert Weakland, the boy Casey, the maid Josie, the artist Paul Funge, and Prof. Eamonn Wall.

Central to four of Liddy's "Territorial Poems" is the concept of the significant anecdote, otherwise known as "gossip": "This information is important, Eric, to the future of American poetry which will be written in this century given the right gossip" (54). So in "The Territory of Enid Starkie and Rimbaud" (35-36), what unites the French poet and his biographer Starkie (who was Irish) is that they both wore sailor suits "on the Seine and on the Thames"; the point is that they "wear sailor suits for beauty not work". Equally well, a point emerges out of the dialogue about love and sex between an unnamed speaker (Liddy?) and Burroughs in "The Territory of William Burroughs" (40-41) – this is the desirability of a young man who can be assimilated to a lizard: "'I want a black lizard with beautiful violet eyes ...'" One of the most gossipy of these poems is "The Territory of Jack Spicer" (44-45): "Jack Spicer was terrible in bed". And again the point: Liddy adapts Tennyson on Virgil[3] – "wielder of the stateliest measure/ever moulded by the lips of man" – to praise Spicer's writing: "most caressing enforcer of paragraphs/ever moulded by the lips of wobblies and cowboys". Another highly anecdotal poem is "The Territory of Michael Hartnett" (49-51). Central here is the poet's drinking: "while Angela/was away his daughter had brought him over/lunch, an orange a bottle of vodka"; "He said to Nuala Ní Dhomhnaill he blamed/Natasha. 'Natasha who?' 'Natasha/Smirnoff'". But his consumption of alcohol is inextricably linked to creativity: "From the day in the kitchen to the day in the/hospital Raifteirí and Merriman two pourers".

Three other territorial poems dealing with Kerouac, Jarry, and Elizabeth Bowen and Medbh McGuckian are more discursive in style. Kerouac for Liddy is one of his poetic trinity with Yeats and Kavanagh, and in the earlier poem "Kerouac's Ronsard Dance" he is identified with Christ, Ronsard, and Liddy himself: "Jesus, Ronsard, Jack, I have become".[4] Since Kerouac saw himself as basically religious, as a "strange solitary crazy Catholic mystic",[5] Liddy uses religious language about him in "The Territory of Kerouac" (42-43): "Salvation is how you sing/and dance on a visit to the Virgin Mary". But such religion must find a place for love: "Love is a Canon Law Code". More, the religion of Kerouac and Liddy is so fully incarnational that it finds a place even for excrement: "If you wish smear me with dung", and as Yeats said, "Love has pitched his mansion in/the place of excrement".[6]

In "The Territory of Jarry" (37-39), what Jarry exhibits in particular is beauty and sexual desire. So Liddy finds "A man so much more beautiful than me", and notes that "the aristos are martyrs for sexlove". But at the same time, Liddy's penchant for ambiguity leads him to infer that Jarry may be his man: "I wed thee I wed thy/womanising body".

In "The Territory of the Planter and the Gael" (46-48), Liddy establishes the difference between the politics and ethnicities of Elizabeth Bowen and Medbh McGuckian. McGuckian is seen as an Irish nationalist, Bowen as a supporter of England during World War II. But Bowen's activities as a low-level spy for England during the war do not make her English. She notes that "'As long as I can remember I've been extremely conscious/of being Irish ... I must say it's a highly disturbing emotion'", so that Liddy comments, "It takes an Irish person to know how difficult it is to be Irish". Then in terms of ethnicity, Bowen belongs to the Anglo-Irish, McGuckian to the native Gaels. But despite these political and ethnic differences, the two women are writers first, devotees of Dionysus who presided over Athenian tragedy ("goat-song"): "Both writers people of the god and the goat". Stylistically, of course, they are different: "I dream in North Cork/of a book written by a she, I dream in the North of a poem without an I". But in the final analysis, both women as representatives of the two traditions must get together; they "take each other's waists as dandies and dervishes./Otherwise no galas du jour for Ireland./Dance we must, dance we have to, even in circles like this".

3

For Liddy, none of the assorted writers who feature in *I Only Know That I Love Strength in My Friends and Greatness* provide examples of what Harold Bloom calls "the anxiety of influence",[7] rather, these writers offer him what may be called "the freedom of influence", because they are, by and large, radical antinomian figures who provide a variety of paradigms for Liddy's own libertarian perspectives. This is true even of Yeats whose unique achievement in poetry might be thought a source of anxiety for someone of Liddy's generation (born 1934). For Liddy is comfortable around Yeats, as we see in the long prose poem "Yeats: New Ways of Falling in Love" (63-71), perhaps for the reason that the two poets can seem very different – Yeats is straight, Protestant, conservative, partly of the nineteenth century, writes in strict verse forms; Liddy is gay, Catholic, liberal, partly of the twenty-first century, writes in free verse.

In "Yeats: New Ways of Falling in Love", Liddy introduces two speakers named Hic and Ille after the manner of Yeats in his poem "Ego Dominus Tuus", from which lines about the anti-self and its fashioning of poetry are indeed quoted at the end of the poem. Ezra Pound suspected that "Ille" was in reality "Willie", i.e. Yeats.[8] We may infer that Ille is here Liddy. While Yeats's character Ribh studies "hatred with diligence",[9] Liddy's Ille studies Yeats's "spells and wishes with great diligence", and rejects criticism of these by contemporary Irish poets. At issue here is the fact that Yeats's Anglo-American critics have ridiculed his constant search for spiritual truth (whenever it might be found), and have been followed by some Irish critics. So Heaney, "the current laureate", speaks of Yeats's "waywardness and eccentric beliefs", blind to the fact that Yeats is "the teacher of religious studies". This blindness ensures that Heaney, who can make use of many writers (*Beowulf* and Virgil's *Eclogues* most recently), does not make use of Yeats. Indeed Liddy goes on to speak the unspeakable: "Seamus can be a dull writer". (Witness some of the poems in *Electric Light*). The inference is clear: for a poet to cut himself off from the spiritual is to abandon the *sprezzatura* that characterizes both Yeats and Liddy. Why hardly any critic (exceptions Desmond Fennell, James Simmons and David Lloyd[10]) seems willing to say such things would provide material for a thesis.

On the other hand, many American writers do appropriate Yeats, such as Robinson Jeffers, John Berryman, Lorine Niedecker, and Theodore Roethke.[11] Jeffers "was the most authentic Yeatsian, Protestant and reactionary like his master". But Jeffers was "sceptical in the midst of a huge urge to transcendence", whereas Yeats was able to draw on Plato and Plotinus to validate his belief in transcendent reality, the immortality of the soul, and reincarnation.[12] So Liddy revises Auden's racist statement about Yeats – "mad Ireland hurt you into poetry"[13] – to read "mad philosophy hurt him into song". At the same time, Yeats was deeply devoted to opposites,[14] the eternal clash between swordsman and saint – "Land of the swings and roundabouts" – and was, as Kenner said, "a part-time Modernist": "He bowed to Modernism, it bowed back".

Niedecker was taken with the romantic Yeats of pastorals such as "The Lake Isle of Innisfree", while Berryman, who "found the Christian self", may have accepted *A Vision*: "was Berryman fully at home with, could he stay in, the moon-run *A Vision*'s heaven and hell?" Yeats is also relevant to Roethke who visited Richard Murphy in the West of Ireland at "Byzantium Pub & Restaurant"[15]: Roethke's energy derives from Yeats's late ballads that exhibit "lust and rage".[16]

Some Irish poets have also given Yeats his due. Kavanagh, though not sympathetic to the Literary Renaissance, saw that Yeats was special: "'One living poem ... can redeem a whole school of writers from death. During the lifetime of Yeats that living poem appeared again and again ...'" Eavan Boland recognized Yeats's absolute commitment to art – "Recognition nothing can stop his singing mouth" – so that in his old age, which he was determined would count,[17] Yeats accepted "humiliation, illumination", and made his exultant spirit triumph over death: "Soul clapping its hands abolished the wake". Even Yeats's "quasi-feudal" world of "ideal peasants, ideal aristocrats and ideal artists" can be redeemed. Medbh McGuckian states that "'I'd almost subscribe to it once the emphasis was on the word ideal'".

Liddy's admiration for Yeats can be inferred from the above, but in the poem he is also fully explicit. Yeats is a kind of encyclopedia of poetry and of Ireland: "Brought up on Yeats – how else would I know anything about poetry or Ireland?" (The political equivalent is Michael Collins).

4

If writing and especially poetry is a pervasive theme in Liddy, so too is religion. This is emphatically not what Liddy calls "cold rain Catholicism",[18] but is rather strongly antinomian, fully accepting of the radical doctrine of Incarnation, celebratory of God and Christ. Discussion of religion in Ireland is nearly always based on the particular form of Roman Catholicism that emerged after the Famine[19] and that is now in its death throes. Because of this obsession, such discussion – whether by supporters or opponents – tends to be puerile in nature. It is part of Liddy's achievement as a poet that he eschews these facile positions and presents an adult view of religion. Here the analogue is not so much Yeats (who had other sources of spiritual enlightenment) as Blake, who may have belonged in London to a radical dissenting group the Muggletonians,[20] and who is a presence in Liddy's poem "Proverbs of Corca Bascinn". Indeed the dictum that "Everything is owed to the devil's party" (53) suggests Blake's view that, in *Paradise Lost*, Milton was "of the Devil's Party without knowing it".[21]

Liddy's Christianity owes something to Wilde, who held that Christ was an artist.[22] Hence Liddy writes of "Christ's uncorrupted face on an Art Centre wall" (56), and asserts that the Pope, in the best traditions of the Renaissance "is the supreme art critic" (75). Indeed Renaissance Popes were not just figures of authority, but were like lowly monks who experience beauty and desire (Cardinal Hume was a monk who championed being in love). But Liddy notes that such figures from the past are no more, adapting a quotation from Marlowe's *The Jew of Malta* (1533), already the epigraph to Eliot's "Portrait of a Lady": "besides these wenches were in another country and were men" (76).

This theme of art and religion is stressed further in the poem "The Cabala" (58-60). Liddy finds that "a consolation to a cardinal in old age is the sensual/dominance of poetry" in the shape of major Latin poets such as Catullus, Horace, Virgil (*Eclogues*), Ovid. Indeed "the good cardinals" wish they had written a poem about the Holocaust. But in the Vatican the contemporary Pope has "no time for poems" and instead writes encyclicals "in less than punchy Latin". (Meanwhile, ordinary Catholics, unaware of the complexities of the lives of Popes and cardinals, punctiliously mark the Pope's birthday.) The reaction to the cardinals, who identify with Christ, is to devote themselves to poetry and to drink (Christ gave us the Beatitudes and turned the water into wine). They produce the radical Blakean paradox that the chief site of Catholicism be termed "Gehenna", which means not only "hell" but also "a prison". The inference is that the liberating message of Christ has become distorted by institutional Christianity which seeks to control people's lifestyles (like all fundamentalist religion).

Drink and religion are again linked in the poem "Late Night Sabbath Note" (12-13). A priest refers to Christ's endorsement of wine at Cana and suggests its liberating force, what Horace calls *libera vina*[23]: "Fr. Mike quotes bartender voice in the Gospel./A good bartender saves the world".

In the poems so far considered, Liddy proceeds in his characteristic mode of affirmation through indirection. But the prose poem "The Lord's Passion, March 24, 2002" (80-81) is tentative and direct, as the author struggles with the mystery of suffering. Since no definitive answer to this problem has been found by theologians and philosophers, we should adopt Keats's notion of "negative capability" – "when man is capable of being in uncertainties, Mysteries, doubts, without any irritable reaching after fact & reason".[24] Hence Liddy's assertion about the suffering, "I tell them it seems we are left but we must keep faith". Faith that requires us to imagine the truth: "I am imagining as usual true religion" (11).

5

In the poem "The Territory of the Planter and the Gael", Liddy issues a crucial programmatic statement:

> I am alien and Dionysian and in my books my house is jammed
> with lovers, I am alien primitive and Dionysian and my poems
> curate portrait galleries where nude lovers flourish. (47)

Dionysus is the god of transformation, of wine, of the theatre, of the mask, of wild nature, of ecstatic religion, of new life at spring, of death and resurrection, of a happy afterlife. Here Dionysus is further seen as the force which presides over poetry and over love, as though he had taken on board the function of Apollo and of Aphrodite in addition to his own. In all this, there is an element of the "alien", a category dear to Liddy's antinomian heart and to his position as a gay man. Yet Apollo has his say – the fashioned poems of *I Only Know That I Love Strength in*

My Friends and Greatness are sufficient proof. And Rimbaud concurs: "Moi whispers at last, 'Under an African sun/Apollo reminisces'" (36).

NOTES

[1] For reader-oriented theory see, e.g., R. Selden, *A Reader's Guide to Contemporary Literary Theory* (Brighton, 1985), 105-27.

[2] James Liddy, *I Only Know That I Love Strength in My Friends and Greatness* (Galway, 2003), 72. Further references to this work will be noted in parentheses in the text.

[3] Tennyson, "To Virgil".

[4] Liddy, *Collected Poems* (Omaha, 1994), 229.

[5] As previously noted in Brian Arkins, *James Liddy: A Critical Study* (Galway, 2001), 13.

[6] Yeats, "Crazy Jane Talks with the Bishop".

[7] Harold Bloom, *The Anxiety of Influence* (Oxford, 1975).

[8] Richard Ellmann, *Yeats: The Man and the Masks* (London, 1965), 201.

[9] Yeats, "Ribh Considers Christian Love Insufficient".

[10] Desmond Fennell, "Whatever You Say, Say Nothing" in his *Heresy: The Battle of Ideas in Modern Ireland* (Belfast, 1993), 130-77; James Simmons, "The Trouble with Seamus" in *Seamus Heaney: A Collection of Critical Essays*, ed. E. Andrews (London, 1992), 39-66; David Lloyd, "'Pap for the Dispossessed': Seamus Heaney and the Poetics of Identity" in his *Anomalous States: Irish Writing and the Postcolonial Moment* (Dublin, 1993), 13-40.

[11] See T.E. Diggory, *Yeats and American Poetry: The Tradition of the Self* (Princeton, 1983).

[12] Brian Arkins, *Builders of My Soul: Greek and Roman Themes in Yeats* (Gerrard's Cross, 1990), 24-69.

[13] W.H. Auden, "In Memory of W.B. Yeats".

[14] See B. Arkins in *Yeats-Eliot Review* 8 (2001): 3-19.

[15] Richard Murphy, *The Kick: A Life among Writers* (London, 2002), 199-207.

[16] Yeats, "The Spur".

[17] "He was determined to make his last years count". R. Ellmann, *Four Dubliners* (London, 1988), 29.

[18] Liddy, "Clare, the Butterflies", *A White Thought in a White Shade* (Dublin, 1987), 96.

[19] T. Brown, *Ireland: A Social and Cultural History 1922-1979* (London, 1981), 27-44.

[20] E.P. Thompson, *Witness against the Beast: William Blake and the Moral Law* (Cambridge, 1994).

[21] Blake, "The Marriage of Heaven and Hell".

[22] B. Arkins, *Rivista di Studi Vittoriani* 8 (1999): 20-21.

[23] Horace, *Ars Poetica*, 85.

[24] Keats, letter to George and Thomas Keats, 21 December 1817.

BRIAN ARKINS is a Professor of Classics at NUI, Galway. He is the author of numerous works of scholarship, among them *Sexuality in Catullus* (Georg Olms Verlag, 1982), *Greek and Roman Themes in Joyce* (The Edwin Mellen Press, 1999) and *James Liddy: A Critical Study* (Arlen House, 2001).

JAMES LIDDY

To Joan Navarre Founding the
Oscar Wilde Society of America

You may not, said Sir Edward Carson to the city cock,
You may not sing of Apollo,
The sun does not shine in England

Or Ireland. The city cock
Kept stuffing the sun into his brandy glass. *Disgusting*,
Cried Sir Edward, *go behind bars!*

I am an artist,
The city cock remarked to Sir Edward,
I will lie in the dark with my bright lines.

previously uncollected

NIALL MCGRATH

To Michael S. Begnal Founding the James Liddy Society of America

You may, said Oscar Wilde to the dandy culchie bard,
You may sing of Dionysus,
The cock oftimes crows in Wexford

Or Wisconsin. The dandy culchie bard
Kept stuffing the cock into his whiskey tumbler. *Lovely,*
Cried Oscar, *Go feast with panthers!*

I am a poet,
The dandy culchie bard remarked to Oscar,
I will recline in the light with my obscure lines.

NIALL MCGRATH is publisher of the Co. Antrim-based Black Mountain Press and *The Black Mountain Review*. His first full-length poetry collection, *Reversion*, appeared in 2003 from Sixties Press. It was followed in 2005 by a chapbook, *Indulgences*, and the verse drama for voices, *Farmer's Year* (both Poetry Monthly Press).

THOMAS DILLON REDSHAW

White Ivy

for James Liddy

Fiddleheads in the road-side ditch
Unfurl the faux-marble feathered
Round the hall to the Swilly lawn
Beyond which steely sands gleam
Through sashes that plait this view
In each pane.

Who remain behind
See the ivied road & wall
Stretch from muntin to muntin
Where each leaf ferries North
Evergreen from leaf to leaf that
Grows a mortar vert & throws
A Flemish bond between relict wood
& new-disced field.

The walker's eye
Variegates each mass of leaf
Wrapping wall, climbing a hedge
From the lemon primrose
In the drain.

In distinction
We seek relief, revelation or
Recreation in exception, until
By brook & culvert, or homely pond
The solitary sees the sport
Of one white leaf

the glistening day
Creates because we keep our distance.

A boatman calls for his skiff
& lifts his lanthorn, trembling

At the lough's dark shore where
Evergreen clothes the worn defile
Of Fort Stewart, whose last arch's decay
Holds soil nourishing the exception
Of a blank leaf,
the white heart.

7/25/04

THOMAS DILLON REDSHAW is Director of the Center for Irish Studies at the University of St. Thomas and editor of the *New Hibernia Review*. He edited the 1971 edition of Thomas MacGreevy's *Collected Poems* (New Writers' Press), and more recently has edited *Well Dreams: Essays on John Montague*, a distinguished collection of critical essays published by Creighton University Press in 2002.

Dennis O'Driscoll

On the Road

This live poem for James Liddy's 70th begins
on the *Cill Dara* bus where I am reading Paul Hoover
on Frank O'Hara in *American Poetry Review.*

"Personism" (*I was realizing that if I wanted to*
I could use the telephone instead of writing the poem)
is the manifesto most favoured on this bus.

The oral poets call home on the cell-phone,
accounting for every movement and for none
(*The traffic's absolutely shit*); young Bashos

of the text message compose lyric ideograms
(*cw2cu*) while the 2 FM Top Twenty charts, channelled
through bus speakers, keep us in suspense.

We have four *climbers and* seven *new entries.*
But what will be the song at this week's Numb-er Ooooone?
Back on the page, my eyes range over O'Hara's lunchtime

beat: he picks up a street-poem as casually as a liver
sausage sandwich. *The push is always toward actuality*
rather than mythology of self, Hoover goes on.

2 FM adds further tension by breaking for commercials.
Hurry, these bargains won't be around forever, you know.
Are there really people whose must-buys include

microfibre jog legs, with side zippers? Then it's action stations.
The traffic starts to move. The charts reach Number Three.
Ringtones – "Sex and the City", "Men Behaving Badly" – go ballistic.

Hills, arranged discreetly behind hills – an art that conceals art –
steal into view, in an evening blur of colours as I step off
the *Cill Dara* (rhyme it with O'Hara) bus, still ignorant

of who made it to the coveted Number One spot.

DENNIS O'DRISCOLL was born in Thurles, Co. Tipperary, in 1954. His seven books of poetry include *Exemplary Damages* (Anvil Press, 2002) and *New & Selected Poems* (Anvil Press, 2004). A selection of his essays and reviews, *Troubled Thoughts, Majestic Dreams* (Gallery Press), was published in 2001. He received a Lannan Literary Award in 1999.

Colette Nic Aodha

Faoi Ghlas

Doras dúnta
gach áit a chasaim
tusa romham
á chur faoi ghlas.

D'oscail mé arís é
ag fiafraí díot
cén treo?
Bláthanna in áit mo shúl.

Shiúil mé ar aghaidh
ag ceapadh gur ar oscailt
a bhí sé
is tú á dhúnadh arís.

Bhí brionglóid agam,
an doras ar oscailt,
ach é ceangailte go docht.
Ar maidin mé ar shiúl

Náire orm
gur thug éinne faoi deara
m'aghaidh scriosta,
baracáid in áit do dhorais.

A curse on those who harassed me at work
on their next bite may they choke,
their every phone call be a hoax,
may they need an undertaker and a priest
before next midsummer feast,
may someone forget to pay Charon,
their flesh and blood be rat infested carrion.

May their every effort end in failure,
unreasonable, dysfunctional, uncouth harasser,
may their every cup fall from the dresser,
their every bicycle be without mud splasher.
Each time they go for a stroll
may they end up eye-deep in a pot hole.

May each month see them up the duff,
their every golden thing turn to fluff,
oh! they who are full of poisonous stuff
may their ill gotten gains go up in a smoking puff.
The curse of poets on their head
for every malicious word they said.

When I think of the threats they uttered
I wish their offspring permanently scuttered,
each penny they earn that they may flutter,
and they unable to talk but stutter.
May every ill settle on their head
and they never rest easy in their bed
for my good name they stole
may they be eternally engulfed in a flaming black hole.

For all the sleepless nights they caused me
may they go completely crazy,
may their only visitor be a flea
and he to bring his extended family.
Be they bad minded, jealous, or malefactors
this poet never forgets her detractors.

COLETTE NIC AODHA was born in 1967. She has published *as Gaeilge* three collections of poetry and one collection of short stories, all with Coiscéim Her first collection in English, *Sundial*, was published to critical acclaim in September 2005 by Arlen House. She received an Arts Council Bursary for Literature in 2005.